BLOND'S CONTRACTS

Farnsworth Edition

S&G SULZBURGER & GRAHAM PUBLISHING, Ltd.
NEW YORK
(800) 366-7086

BLOND'S CONTRACTS

Farnsworth Edition

by

Neil C. Blond

Louis Petrillo

Farnsworth Edition
revised and edited
by

William Carstanjen

Cynthia Lee

Also Available in this Series:

Blond's Administrative Law
Blond's Civil Procedure
Blond's Constitutional Law
Blond's Contracts
Blond's Corporate Tax
Blond's Corporations
Blond's Criminal Law
Blond's Criminal Procedure
Blond's Essay Questions — Contracts
Blond's Essay Questions — Torts
Blond's Evidence
Blond's Family Law
Blond's Income Tax
Blond's International Law
Blond's Multistate Questions
Blond's Professional Responsibility Questions
Blond's Property
Blond's Torts

Reprinted 1994

ISBN 0-945819-27-7

How To Use This Book

"You teach yourself the law, we teach you how to think"
- Professor Kingsfield, The Paper Chase

Law school is very different from your previous educational experiences. In the past, course material was presented in a straightforward manner both in lectures and texts. You did well by memorizing and regurgitating. In law school, your fat casebooks are stuffed with material, most of which will be useless when finals arrive. Your professors ask a lot of questions but don't seem to be teaching you either the law or how to think. Sifting through voluminous material seeking out the important concepts is a hard, time-consuming chore. We've done that job for you. This book will help you study effectively. We hope to teach you the law and how to think.

Preparing for class

Most students start their first year by reading and briefing all their cases. They spend too much time copying unimportant details. After finals they realize they wasted time on facts that were useless on the exam.

Case Clips

This book contains a case clip of every major case covered in your casebook. Case Clips help you focus on what your professor wants you to get out of your cases. Case Clips are written in a way that should provide a tremendous amount of understanding in a relatively short period of time. Facts, Issues, and Rules are carefully and succinctly stated. Left out are details irrelevant to what you need to learn from the case. In general, we skip procedural matters in lower courts. We don't care which party is the appellant or petitioner because the trivia is not relevant to the law. Case Clips should be read before you read the actual case. You will have a good idea what to look for in the case, and appreciate the significance of what you are reading. Inevitably you will not have time to read all your cases before class. Case Clips allow you to prepare for class in about five minutes. You will be able to follow the discussion and listen without fear of being called upon.

Hanau Charts

When asked how he managed to graduate in the top ten percent of his class at one of the ten most prestigious law schools in the land,

Paul Hanau introduced his system of flow charts now known as Hanau Charts.

A very common complaint among first year students is that they "can't put it all together." When you are reading 400 pages a week it is difficult to remember how the last case relates to the first and how November's readings relate to September's. It's hard to understand the relationship between different torts topics when you have read cases for three or four other classes in between. Hanau Charts will help you put the whole course together. They are designed to help you memorize fundamentals. They reinforce your learning by showing you the material from another perspective.

Outlines

More than one hundred lawyers and law students were interviewed as part of the development of this series. Most complained that their casebooks did not teach them the law and were far too voluminous to be useful before an exam. They also told us that the commercial outlines they purchased were excellent when used as hornbooks to explain the law, but were too wordy and redundant to be effective during the weeks before finals. Few students can read four 500-page outlines during the last month of classes. It is virtually impossible to memorize that much material and even harder to decide what is important. Almost every student interviewed said he or she studied from homemade outlines. We've written the outline you should use to study.

"But writing my own outline will be a learning experience."

True, but unfortunately many students spend so much time outlining they don't leave time to learn and memorize. Many students told us they spent six weeks outlining, and only one day studying before each final!

Mnemonics

Most law students spend too much time reading, and not enough time memorizing. Mnemonics are included to help you organize your essays and spot issues. They highlight what is important and which areas deserve your time.

TABLE OF CONTENTS

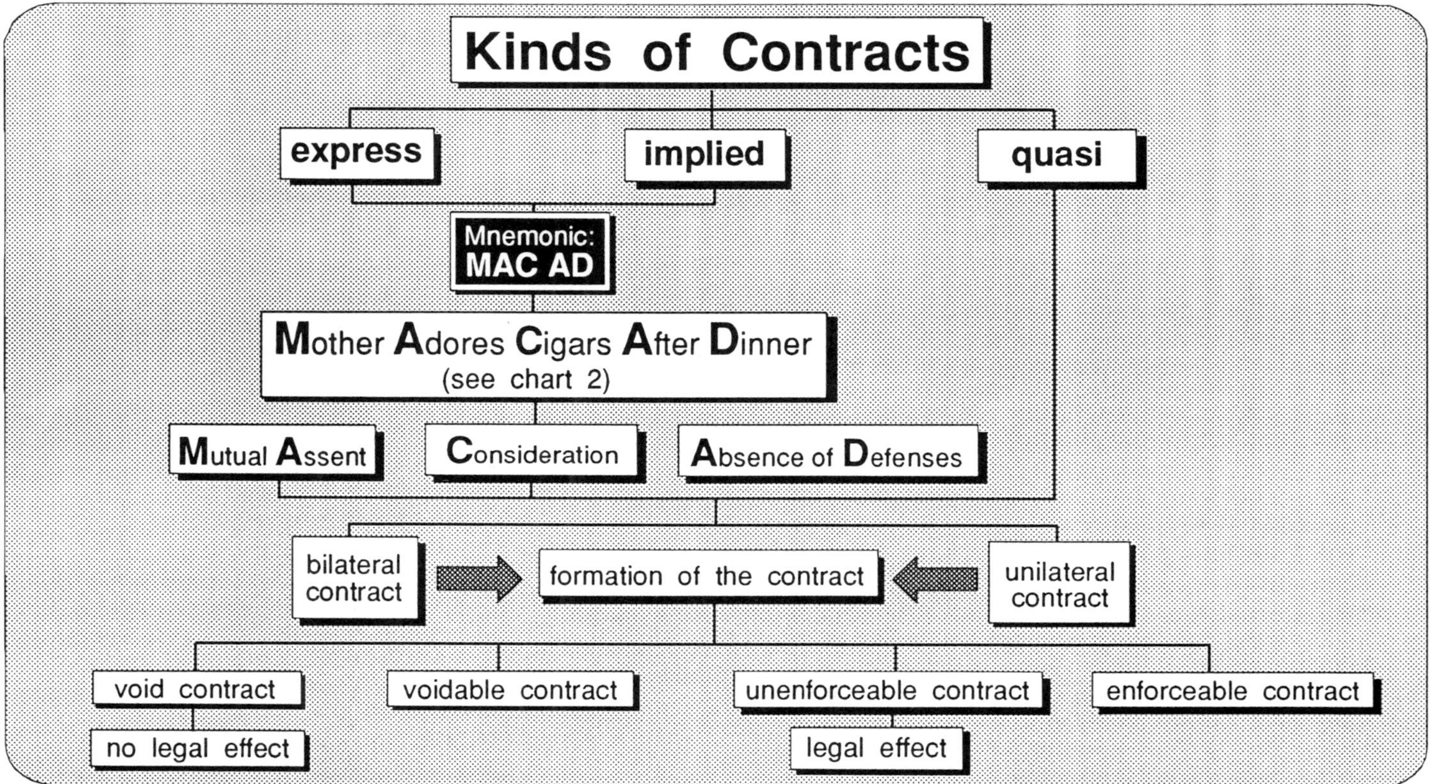

Hanau Chart 1

Blond's Contracts

Hanau Chart 2

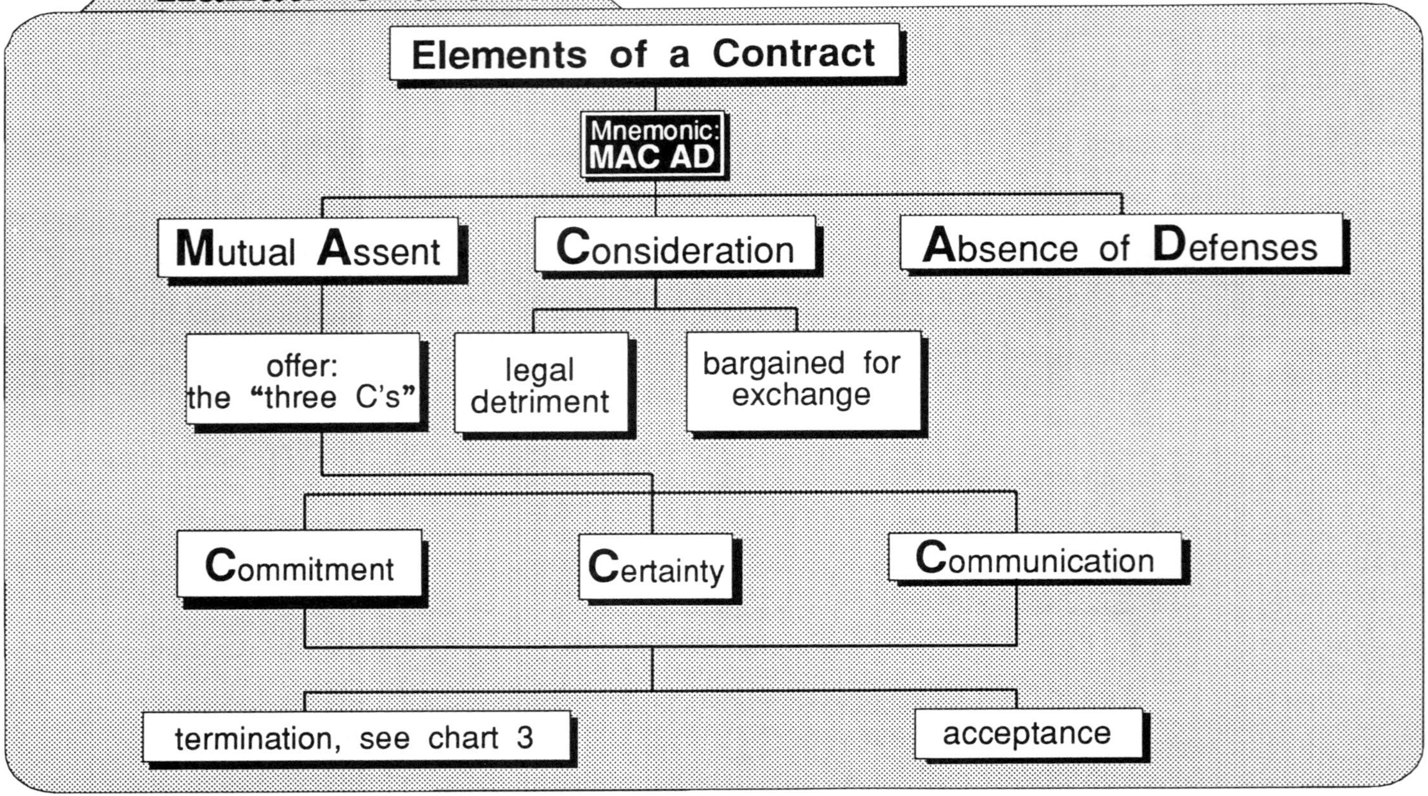

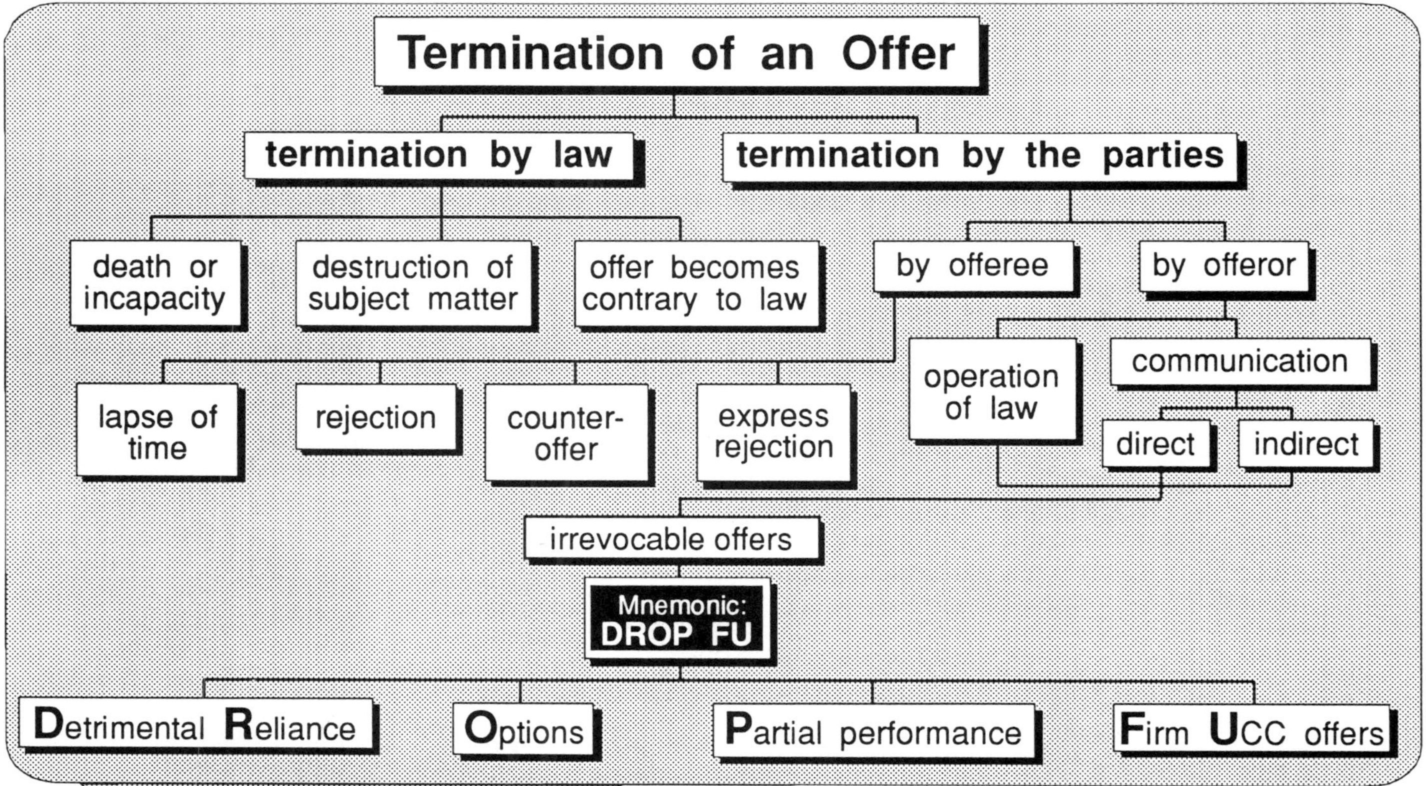

Hanau Chart 3

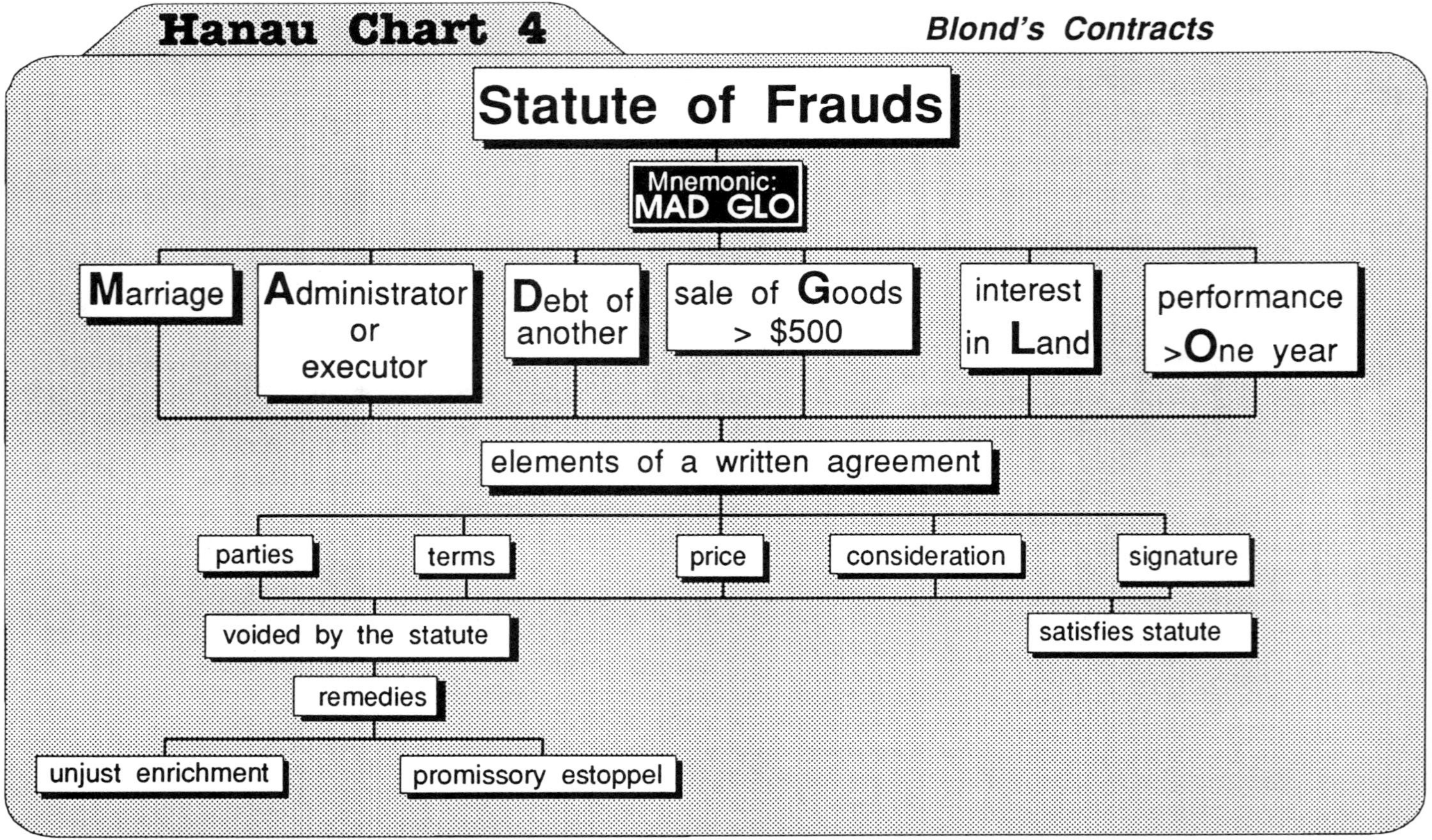
Hanau Chart 4
Statute of Frauds
Mnemonic: MAD GLO
Marriage
Administrator or executor
Debt of another
sale of Goods > $500
interest in Land
performance >One year
elements of a written agreement
parties
terms
price
consideration
signature
voided by the statute
satisfies statute
remedies
unjust enrichment
promissory estoppel

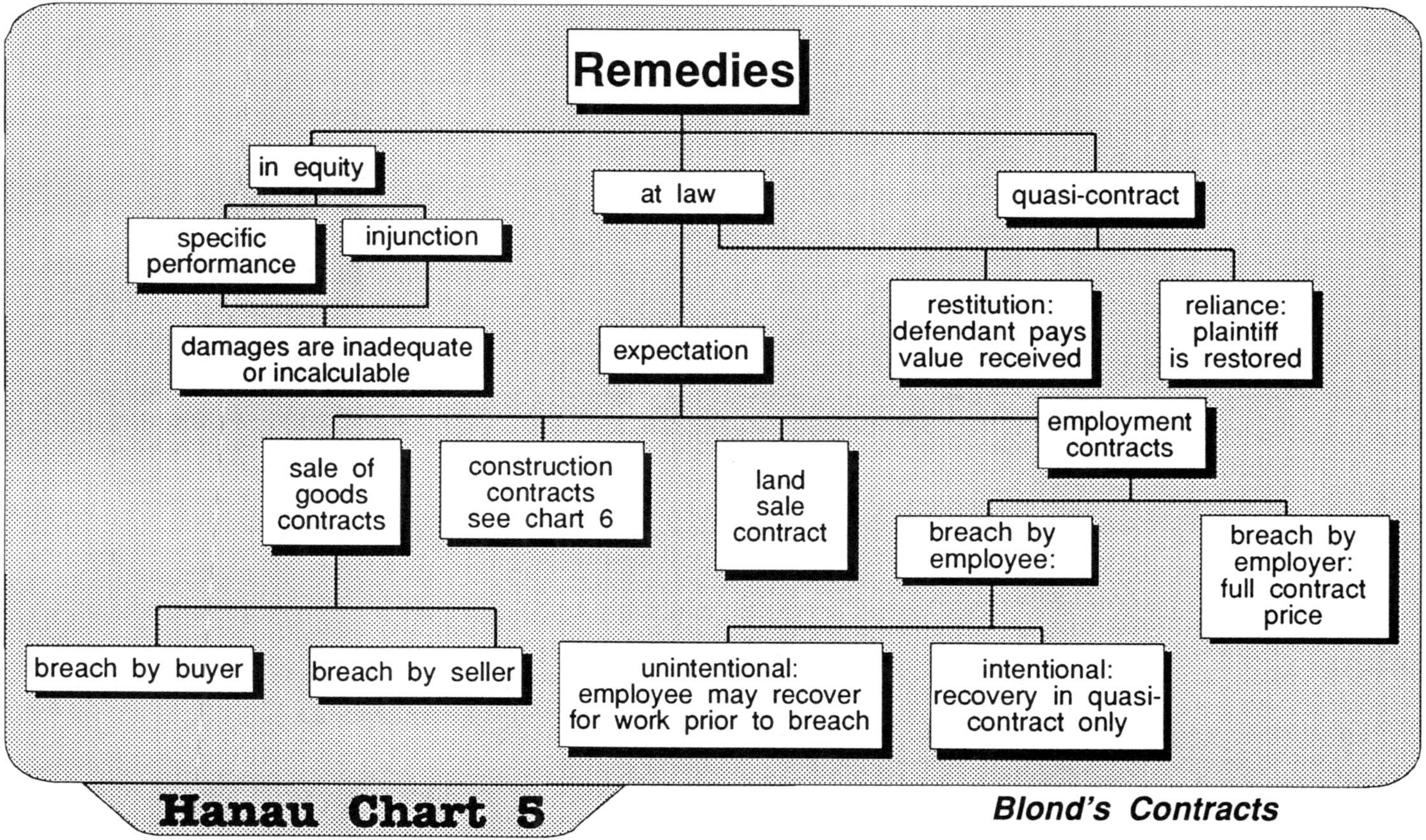

Hanau Chart 5

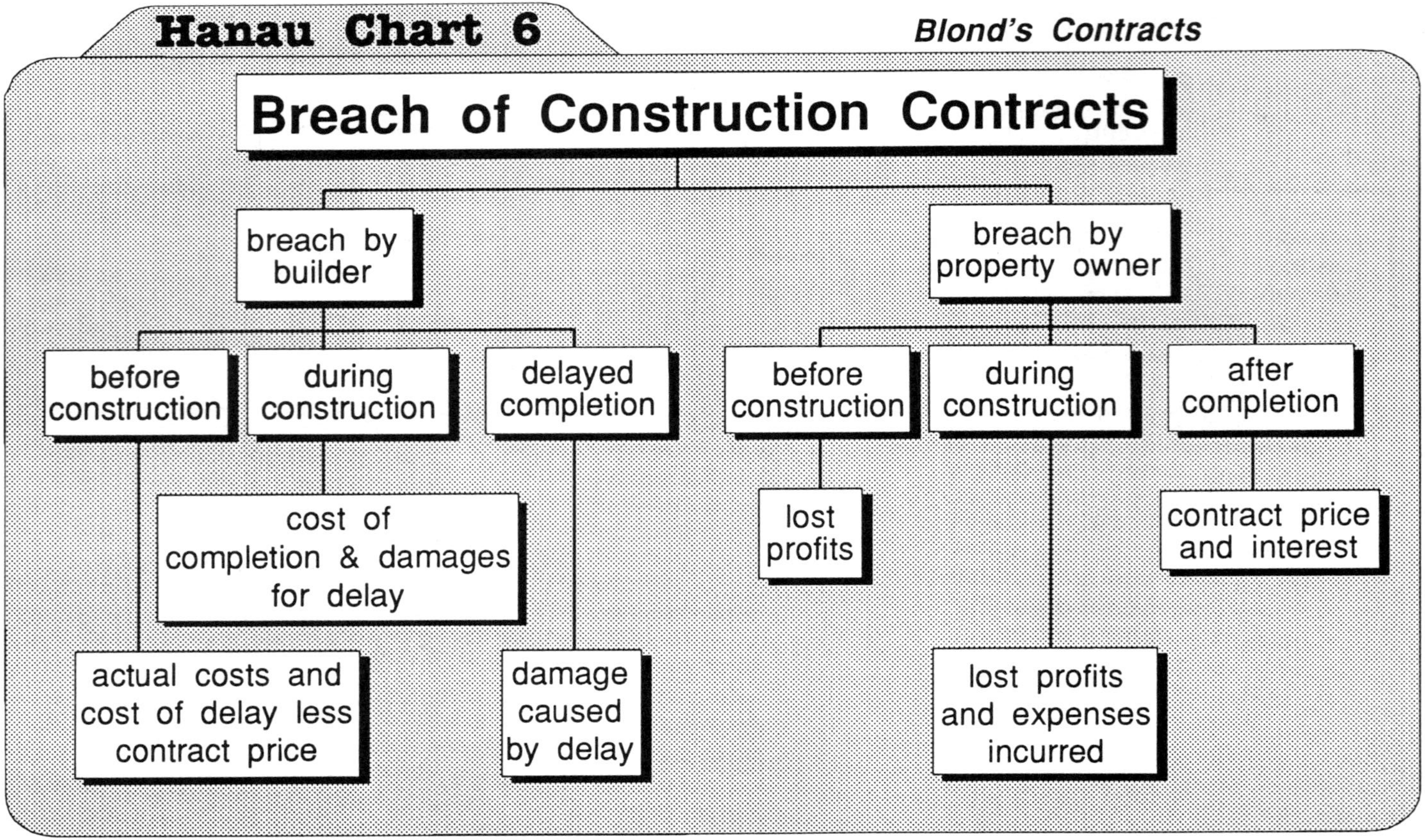
Hanau Chart 6
Blond's Contracts
Breach of Construction Contracts
breach by builder
breach by property owner
before construction
during construction
delayed completion
before construction
during construction
after completion
cost of completion & damages for delay
lost profits
contract price and interest
actual costs and cost of delay less contract price
damage caused by delay
lost profits and expenses incurred

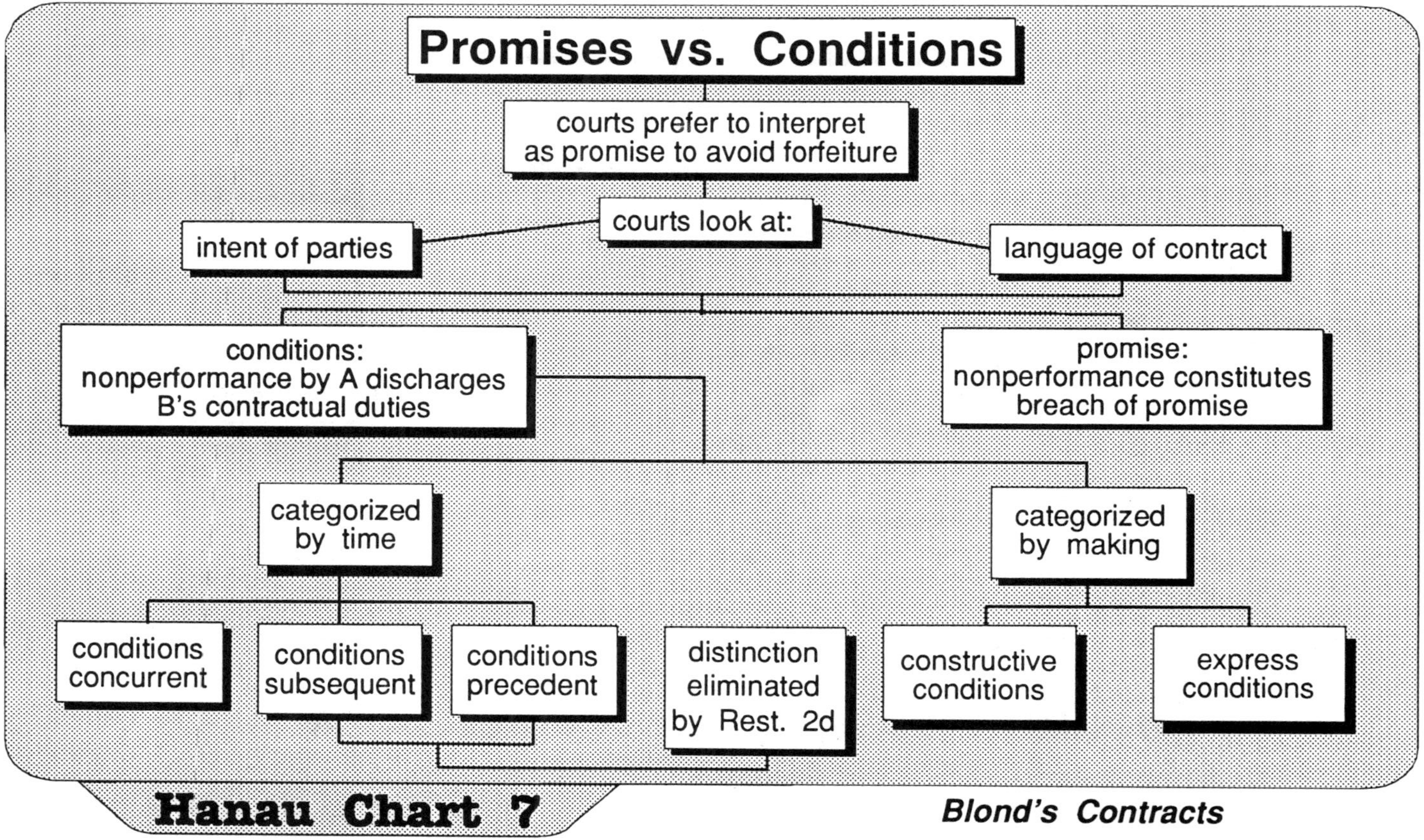
Promises vs. Conditions
courts prefer to interpret as promise to avoid forfeiture
courts look at:
intent of parties
language of contract
conditions: nonperformance by A discharges B's contractual duties
promise: nonperformance constitutes breach of promise
categorized by time
categorized by making
conditions concurrent
conditions subsequent
conditions precedent
distinction eliminated by Rest. 2d
constructive conditions
express conditions
Hanau Chart 7
Blond's Contracts

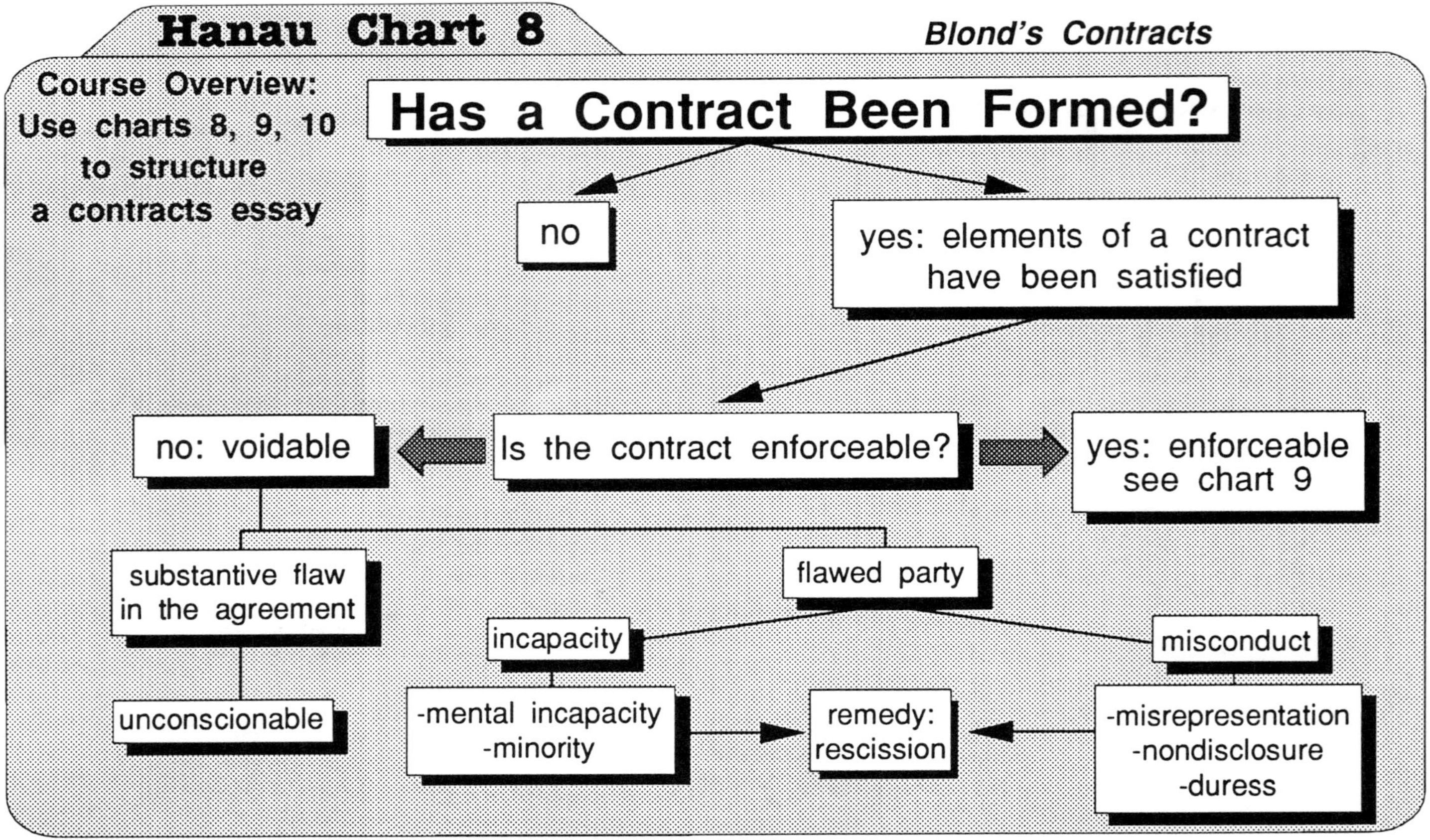
Hanau Chart 8
Blond's Contracts
Course Overview:
Use charts 8, 9, 10
to structure
a contracts essay
Has a Contract Been Formed?
no
yes: elements of a contract have been satisfied
Is the contract enforceable?
no: voidable
yes: enforceable see chart 9
substantive flaw in the agreement
flawed party
unconscionable
incapacity
misconduct
-mental incapacity
-minority
remedy: rescission
-misrepresentation
-nondisclosure
-duress

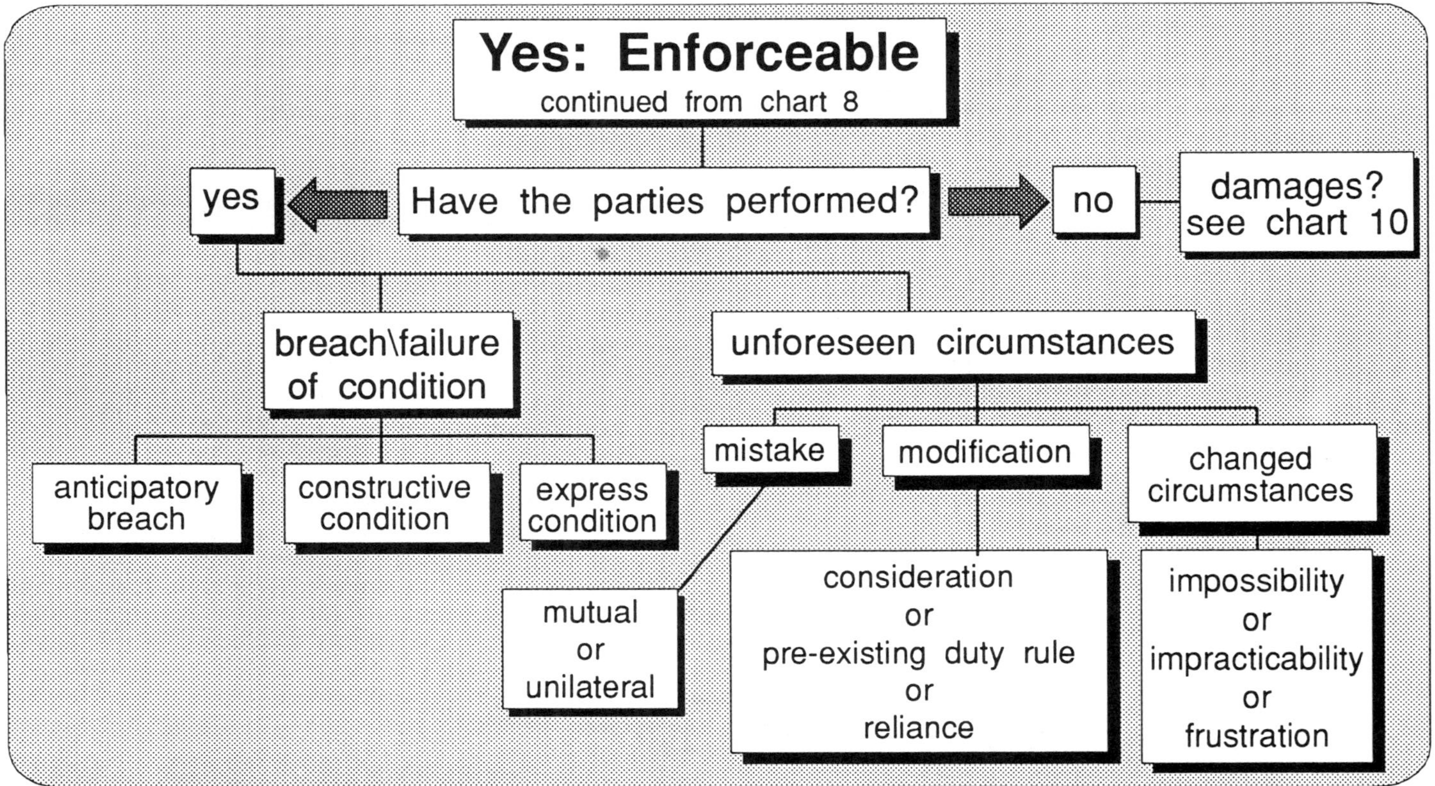

Hanau Chart 9

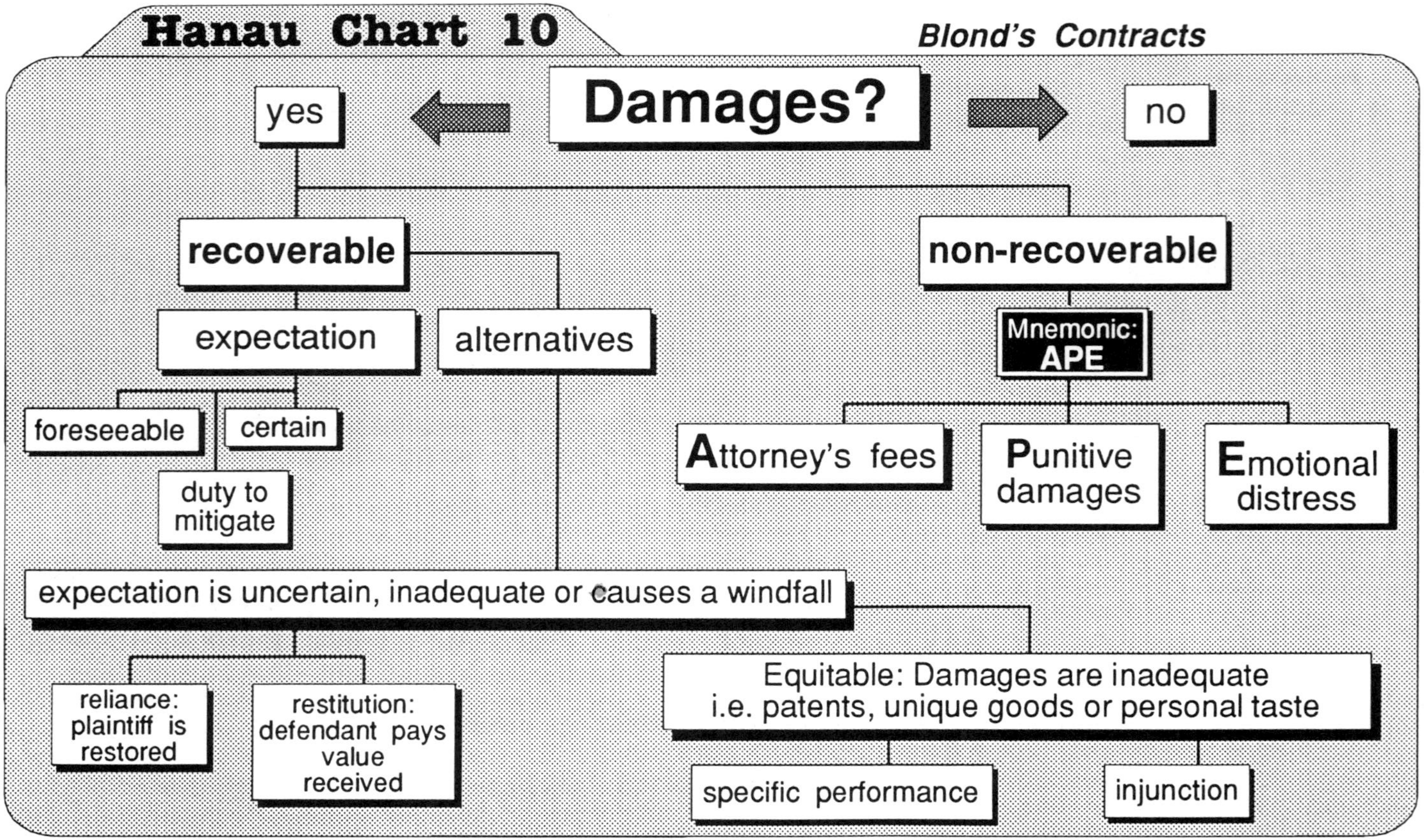
Hanau Chart 10
Blond's Contracts
Damages?
yes
no
recoverable
non-recoverable
expectation
alternatives
foreseeable
certain
duty to mitigate
Mnemonic: APE
Attorney's fees
Punitive damages
Emotional distress
expectation is uncertain, inadequate or causes a windfall
reliance: plaintiff is restored
restitution: defendant pays value received
Equitable: Damages are inadequate i.e. patents, unique goods or personal taste
specific performance
injunction

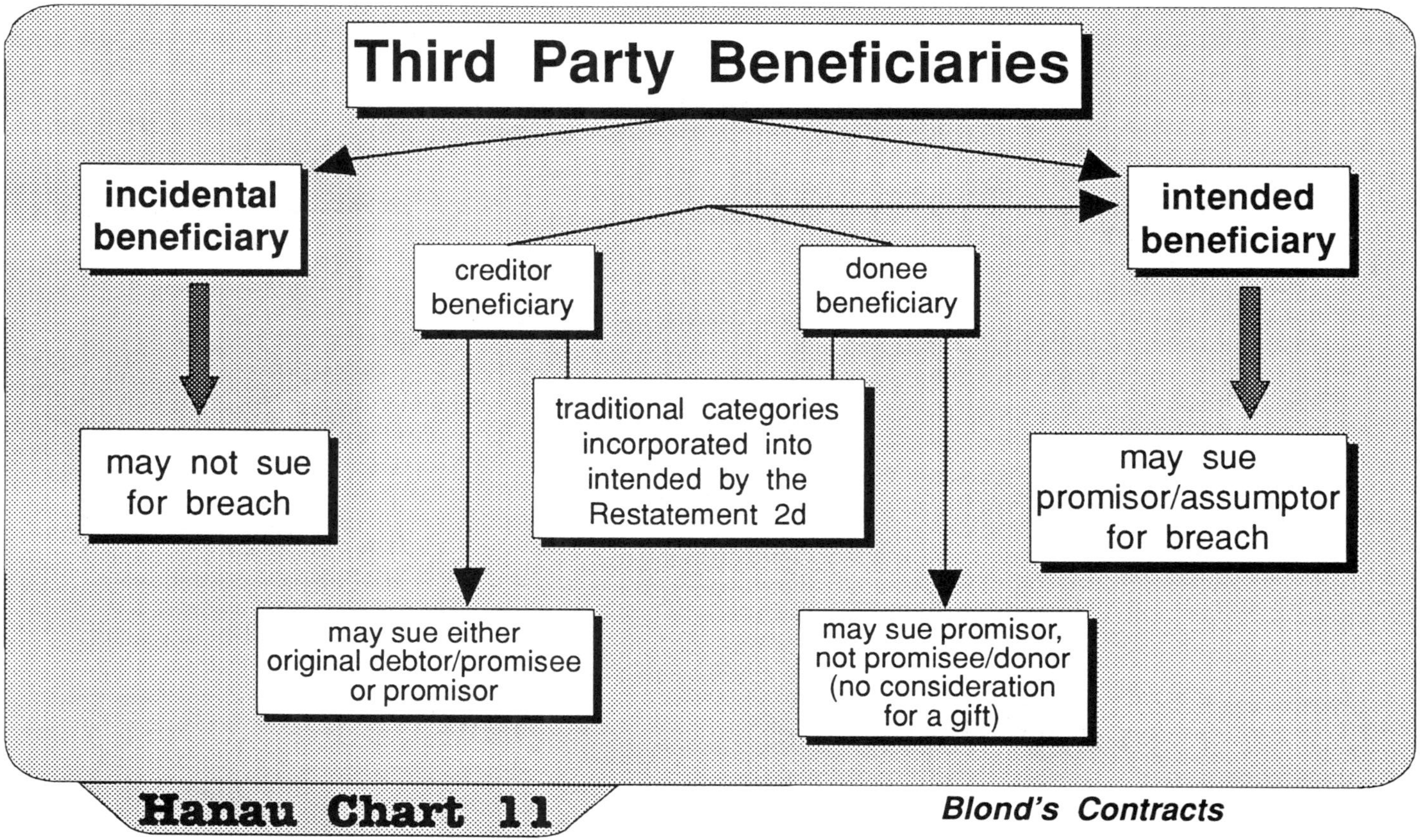

Blond's Contracts

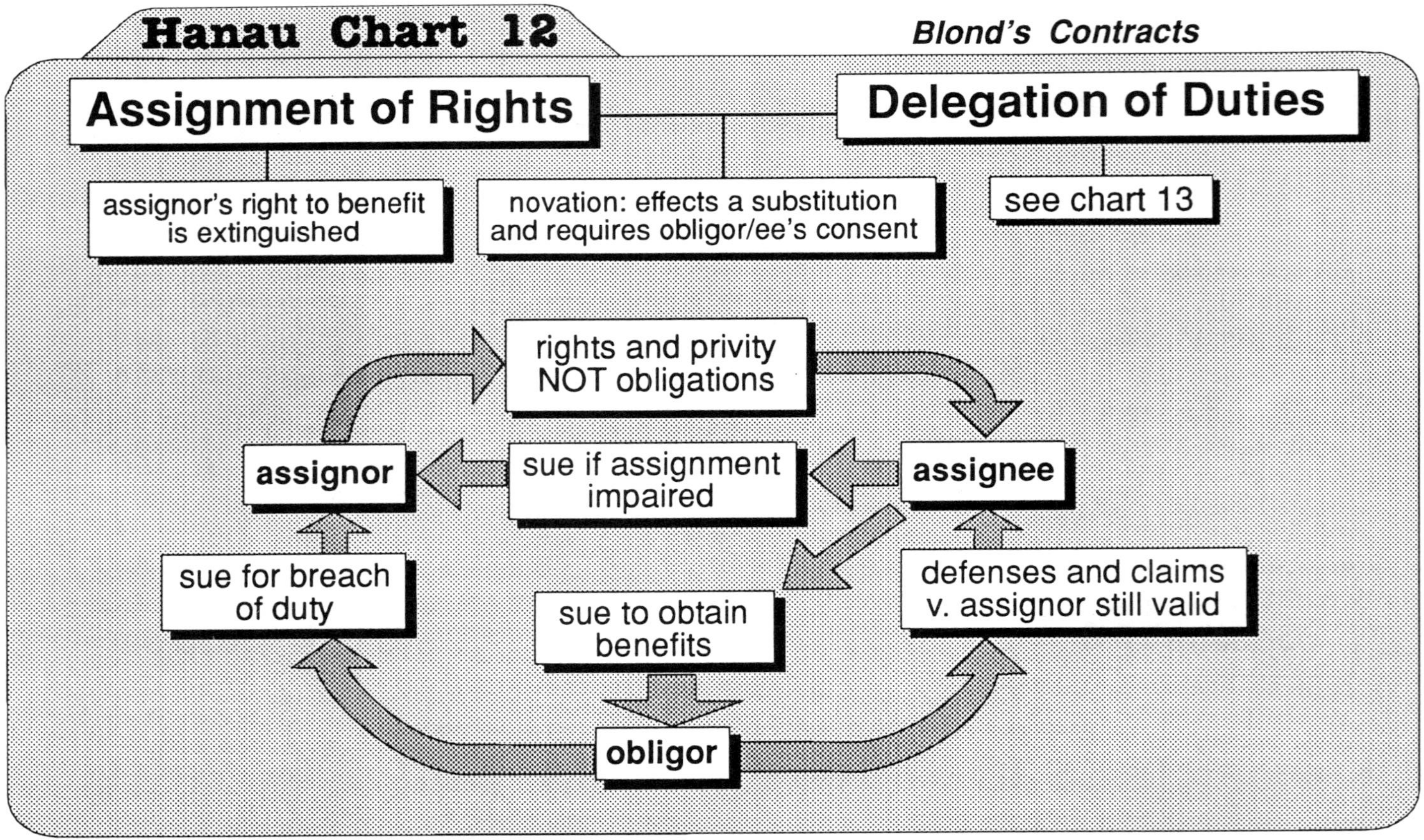
Hanau Chart 12
Blond's Contracts
Assignment of Rights
Delegation of Duties
assignor's right to benefit is extinguished
novation: effects a substitution and requires obligor/ee's consent
see chart 13
rights and privity NOT obligations
assignor
sue if assignment impaired
assignee
sue for breach of duty
sue to obtain benefits
defenses and claims v. assignor still valid
obligor

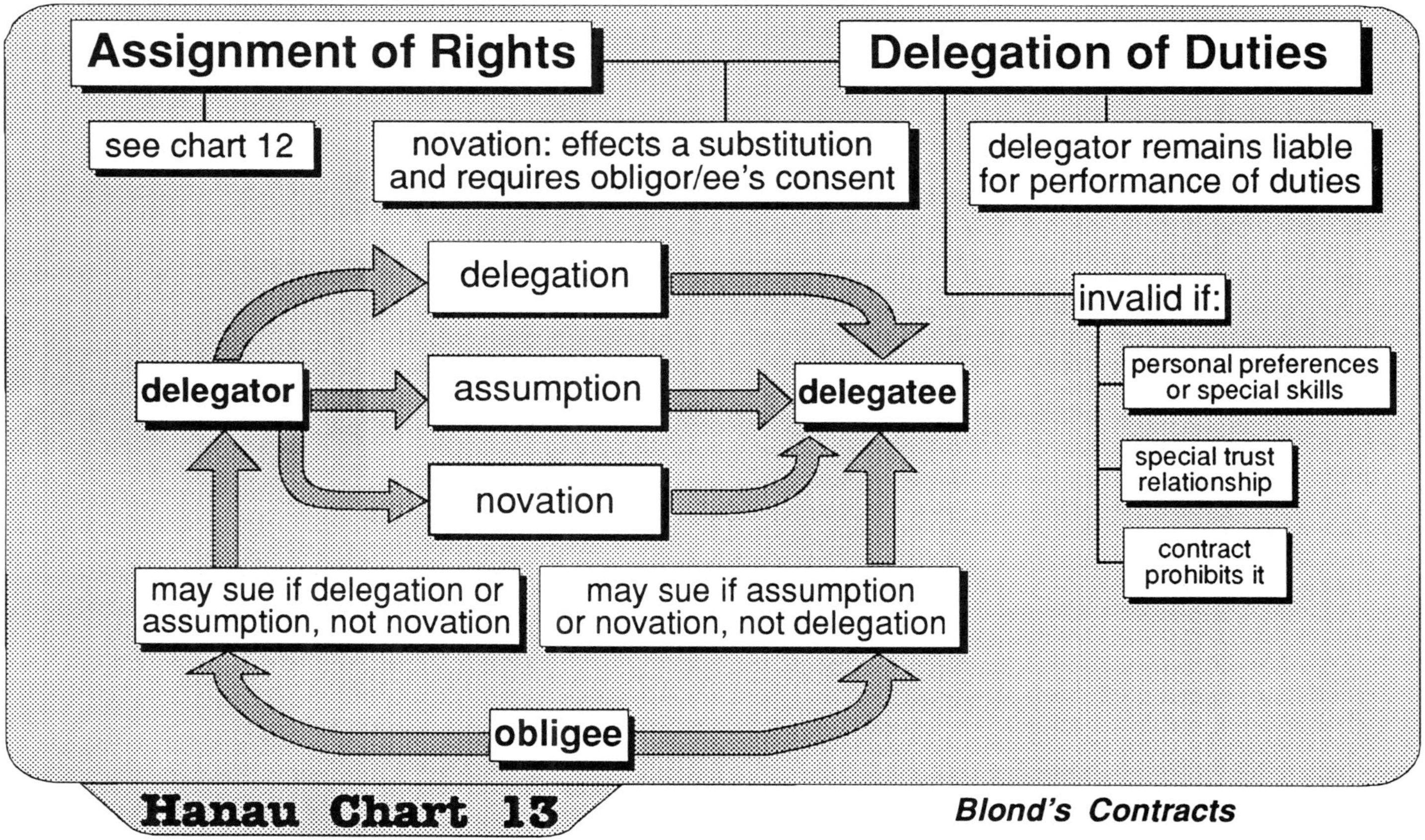

Blond's Contracts

Chapter 1

BASIS FOR ENFORCING PROMISES

I. THE MEANING OF "ENFORCE"

A. Contract Defined

There is no universally accepted definition of a contract, but, in general, a contract is a promissory agreement that is legally enforceable. However, some contracts are unenforceable or voidable under certain circumstances, and others can be formed without an actual agreement (e.g., quasi-contracts).

B. Kinds of Contracts

1. Express
   An express contract is formed by written or oral language.

2. Implied in Fact
   An implied-in-fact contract is manifested by the actions of the parties, although it is not explicitly written or stated. Example: plunking down 50 cents at a newsstand and taking a paper.

3. Implied in Law (quasi-contract)
   A quasi-contract is a recovery or obligation that is not created by an actual agreement, but by the law for "reasons of justice." It is not an actual contract negotiated by the parties. Example: A plumber walks by a home and fixes a burst pipe that was flooding the basement while the home-owner was absent. The plumber may be able to recover in quasi-contract, notwithstanding the absence of an actual agreement with the owner to perform the service and receive compensation.

4. Unilateral-Bilateral Distinction

a. Bilateral Contract
A bilateral contract is formed by mutual exchange of promises by the contracting parties. Example: A promises B that he will sell B ten baseball cards, and B promises to pay A one dollar.

b. Unilateral Contract
A unilateral contract is one in which a promise is made in exchange for actual performance, as opposed to a promise to perform. Example: A promises to pay B $100 if B paints A's home. A has not asked B for a promise to paint, but rather to actually paint.

c. Distinction Between Unilateral and Bilateral Contracts
The difference between unilateral and bilateral contracts is not as important today as in the past. However, one significant difference is the extent of the obligations they impose. Once parties exchange promises in bilateral contracts they are obligated to perform their promises. In a unilateral contract, the nonpromising party is not obligated to perform and the promisor's obligation does not arise until the requested act is completed.

C. Validity of Contracts

1. Enforceable
An enforceable contract is a normal contract that has legal effect.

2. Void
A void contract has no legal effect. Example: a contract to commit crime.

3. Voidable
A voidable contract has legal effect unless one party (e.g., a minor) chooses to void it.

4. Unenforceable

An unenforceable contract is one that has some legal status but no conventional means for a party to assert his rights. Example: The statute of limitations precludes a party from bringing an action in court after a specified time period has elapsed. While corrective measures cannot make a void contract enforceable, an unenforceable contract can sometimes be validated by corrective action of the parties (e.g., memorializing an agreement in writing to satisfy the Statute of Frauds).

D. Equitable Remedies

Although the standard relief for breach of contract is monetary damages, they may be inappropriate in certain situations, such as where the amount of damages is too speculative or the contract was for unique goods. In such cases, courts will grant primarily two forms of equitable relief: injunctions and specific performance. Originally, there were two court systems, law and equity. Today, the distinction has been abolished and all courts can grant either form of remedy. A primary consideration in granting equitable relief is the issue of justice and fairness (treated in more detail in Chapter 4).

E. Sources of Law

1. Common Law

Contract law has traditionally been governed by common law (case law), although many important areas have been superseded by statute in recent years.

2. Uniform Commercial Code

All states except Louisiana have largely adopted the provisions of the Uniform Commercial Code (UCC), which governs many aspects of various commercial transactions. Article 2, which governs sales, is the section of primary importance to basic contracts courses.

3. Restatements

A persuasive but not binding source of contract law is the Second Restatement of Contracts of 1980, which replaced the 1932 Restatement of Contracts. It is an annotated summary of common law by the American Law Institute. However, the law in a given jurisdiction is not necessarily that propounded by the Restatement.

F. Requirements of a Contract

Mnemonic: **Mother Adores Cigars After Dinner**

a) Mutual Assent
b) Consideration
c) Absence of Defenses

II. CONSIDERATION

It would be unfair for courts to hold people to every promise that they make because many promises are made in jest or without sufficient forethought. Thus, to be legally enforceable, a promise must be made in return for *consideration*, which consists of two general elements: *bargained-for exchange* and *legal detriment.*

A. Bargained-for Exchange

A performance or return promise is bargained-for if it is sought by the promisor in exchange for his promise, **and** it is given by the promisee in exchange for that promise. (Rest. 2d. § 71(2).) The bargain requirement serves the purpose of distinguishing between enforceable promises and ordinary gifts.

1. Gifts

A promise to make a gift is unenforceable, not only because it is not bargained for but also because the offeree suffers no legal detriment. Example: A says to B, "I promise to buy you a new car." A is not legally bound to buy B a car because A's promise was not made as part of a bargain in exchange for some return benefit from B. There is no consideration for A's promise.

2. Bargain v. Precondition
   Performance of a bargain benefits the promisor and therefore is valid consideration. Performance of a precondition does not benefit the promisor and is not consideration. Example: X promises his sister a place to raise her family if she comes to visit him. She incurs the expense of moving, but X changes his mind. X is not legally bound to keep his promise, because no consideration was given for it. The moving expenses were incurred as a precondition to fulfilling his request. X did not bargain that he would give his sister a place to stay in exchange for her incurring moving expenses.

3. Benefit

   a. The benefit a promisor receives as part of a bargain does not have to be economic in nature. Example: A promises B $100 if B does not smoke.

   b. However, the benefit must be more than just altruistic pleasure or love. Example: There is no consideration if A promises to pay B's debts as a gesture of gratitude for all the happiness B has given A. Moral obligation does not constitute legal consideration.

4. Adequacy of Consideration

   a. Nominal Consideration
      Often an agreement between two parties will state something like "A promises B . . . in consideration of $1.00 paid to A." Although courts will not ordinarily examine the adequacy of consideration, courts will do so in cases involving purely token consideration, in order to thwart attempts to make gratuitous promises appear legally enforceable. Nominal or sham consideration is usually evidence that a gift is masquerading as a bargained-for exchange.

b. Recited Consideration

A majority of courts allow a promisor who is opposing enforcement of a contract to prove that the consideration recited in the agreement was not actually given. Nonpayment of recited consideration may be used as partial evidence that there was no bargained-for exchange.

c. Past Consideration

As a general rule, "past consideration is no consideration." Logically, a current promise cannot be bargained in exchange for some benefit that the promisor has already received. Example: A promises to pay B, A's employee, $100 a week "in consideration" of B's many years of hard work, or A promises to pay B $1,000,000 after B saves A's life. In both cases A has received the benefit before he made the promise, and, thus, nothing was actually given in exchange for the promise. There are some exceptions to the general rule:

i. Pre-existing Debt

A promise to repay a pre-existing debt that was excused because of a technical defense, such as the running of the statute of limitations, is enforceable without consideration. (Rest. 2d. §§ 82, 83.)

ii. New Promise for Benefits Received

A new promise to pay for benefits received will sometimes be enforceable without consideration on grounds of moral obligation to prevent injustice. (Rest. 2d. § 86.)

B. Legal Detriment

The second requirement for valid consideration is that it must constitute a legal detriment to the promisee. Legal detriment is liberally construed to mean either a promise to do something that one is not legally obligated to do (e.g., cross the street) or to refrain from doing something that one has a right to do (e.g., stop smoking). There is no requirement that the promisee suffer any actual hardship. Likewise, the benefit that the promisor receives is not necessarily related to pleasure or advantage. All that is required is that the promisor does something he does not have to do.

1. Minority View
   Some courts broaden the test such that valid consideration exists if the promisor received a benefit, even if the promisee did not "suffer" a detriment.

2. Bilateral Contract
   In a bilateral contract, the detriment is in the form of a promise.

3. Unilateral Contract
   In a unilateral contract, the detriment is in the form of an action. No consideration exists prior to performance.

4. Pre-existing Duty Rule
   Generally, there is no legal detriment if a party promises to do something that he is already obligated to do, or forbears from doing something that he is not legally entitled to do. (Rest. 2d. § 73.) Example: A promises not to use illegal drugs. Many courts dislike the pre-existing duty rule and have avoided its application in many ways. A promise to perform an act that one is already legally obligated to do may be consideration under certain circumstances.

   Mnemonic: **DUCk PiNS**

   a. Dispute
      If there is an honest dispute as to whether the promisor is already legally obligated to do the promised act, the promise or act may be consideration.

   b. Unforeseen Circumstances
      Unforeseen circumstances make it "fair and equitable" to allow a promisor to modify an agreement without giving new consideration. (Rest. 2d. § 89.)

c. Pre-existing Duty to a Third Party
The promise is made to a third party outside the contract. Example: A contracts with B to construct an elevator in the building that B is erecting for C. B quits the job, but A promises C that he will continue the job if C pays him. The promise is enforceable, even though A already had a legal obligation to build.

d. New or Different Consideration Promised
Even a slight change in the terms of a pre-existing duty will satisfy the requirement of consideration.

e. Sale of Goods
Under UCC § 2-209, which applies only to the sale of goods, modifications of existing contracts can be made without new consideration.

5. Partial Payment as Satisfaction of a Debt
A promise to pay part of a debt, instead of the whole, is not consideration for a return promise by the creditor to relinquish the debt, because the debtor is obligated to pay anyway ("pre-existing duty"). This rule, however, has been overruled by the UCC and by some jurisdictions. Also, courts will consider a promise of partial payment to be valid consideration if;

a. The payment terms are slightly changed.

b. The debtor refrains from declaring bankruptcy.

c. There is an honest dispute as to the debt.

d. A check marked "payment in full" is cashed.

i. At common law, a creditor forfeited no rights to the rest of the debt still outstanding.

ii. Under the UCC, the entire debt is discharged unless a creditor expressly reserves his rights by writing "with recourse," or something to that effect, on the check. (UCC § 1-207.)

6. Forbearance to Bring Suit
   A promise not to sue, made in exchange for some return benefit, is valid consideration if either;

   a. The claim was valid, or

   b. The claim was not valid, and

      i. The parties reasonably believed the claim was valid (majority rule), or

      ii. The validity was uncertain or the promisor subjectively believed that it was valid (Rest. 2d. § 74).

C. Mutuality
Mutuality requires that *each* party to a contract must provide consideration to the other in exchange for the other's promise.

1. Illusory Promises
   An illusory promise is not sufficient consideration, because it only appears to bind the promisor when, in fact, it commits him to nothing at all. (Rest. 2d. § 77.) Example: A promises to be B's agent. B agrees, but reserves the right to terminate at any time. There is no mutuality, because A received no consideration for his promise.

2. Alternative Promises
   A promise that allows the promisor to choose among several alternative performances will satisfy mutuality only if each alternative has valid consideration. (Rest. 2d. § 77.)
   Example: A promises to give B either $1,000 or his car in exchange for B's car. The promise is enforceable because both alternatives embody valid consideration.

3. Right to Withdraw from the Agreement

   A promise that gives the promisor the right to terminate the agreement can still be valid consideration for a return promise if:

   a. Termination is allowed after performance is rendered.

      Example: A promises to be B's agent. B accepts (promises to hire A) but reserves the right to fire A upon 30 days notice. B's promise is consideration for A's promise because the agency agreement must last at least 30 days before B can fire A.

   b. Termination is dependent on ability to perform.

      Example: A promises to sell his house to B. B promises to buy subject to his ability to obtain financing. B's promise satisfies mutuality because it is not dependent on his willingness to perform but rather on his ability.

   c. Termination occurs with notice.

      If the only limitation on termination is the requirement that notice be given, modern courts are likely to recognize such a promise as valid consideration. Some courts will even go so far as to imply a notice requirement, the idea being that if notice is required, performance must occur for the notice period, at least. Example: A promises to clean B's house in exchange for $100 a day, subject to A's right to terminate with seven days notice. The promise is valid consideration because A must perform for at least seven days.

4. Voidable Promises

   A promise that is voidable at a party's election (promises made by minors, incompetents, etc. are voidable if the promisor so chooses) is valid consideration and satisfies the requirement of mutuality. (Rest. 2d. § 78.)

5. Conditional Promises

   A promise that makes performance of an act dependent on the occurrence of a future event is valid consideration if;

a. Condition is Outside Promisor's Control
There is valid consideration, even if a promisor eventually does not have to perform, unless the promisor knows that the condition cannot occur. Example: A promises to pay B $100 for her baseball glove if it rains on Tuesday. This is valid consideration even if it does not rain on Tuesday.

b. Condition is Partially Within Promisor's Control
A court will imply such a promise to mean that the promisor will use reasonable efforts to satisfy the condition. Example: B promises to sell his house to A if he can find a new house within a year. If A agrees, B's promise will be construed to mean that B will make best efforts to find a new home. Otherwise, B's promise is illusory.

6. Option Contracts
A promisee who receives an irrevocable offer (an option contract or a firm offer) is not always required to give consideration in exchange for that offer. (Rest. 2d. § 87; UCC § 2-205.) Even in cases where consideration is recited, courts do not require that it be paid.

7. Requirements and Output Contracts

a. Traditional Rule
A promise to buy goods from a specific seller over a period of time was insufficient consideration for the return promise to supply those goods, if the quantity term was to be determined by what the buyer required over that period (as opposed to a preset amount). Mutuality was lacking because, although the seller had to provide the goods, the buyer did not have to buy if he required nothing.

b. Modern/UCC Rule
Such promises are valid consideration and do not lack mutuality of obligation. UCC § 2-306 implies that the

buyer has a good faith duty to . . .

i. Maintain reasonable requirement levels,

ii. Buy exclusively from that seller, and

iii. Not take advantage of the seller by increasing demand to benefit from fluctuating market prices.

c. Output Contract
Seller promises all of his output to one buyer. A mutuality problem exists because the seller never promised to have any output, let alone a certain amount. Such contracts are now valid because UCC § 2-306 implies that sellers have a good faith duty to maintain a certain level of output.

d. Unilateral Contract
Part performance of a unilateral contract is sufficient consideration to keep a promise open, even though the promisee is not obligated to complete performance. Once part performance is rendered, however, the promisor cannot withdraw his promise unless promisee rejects.

III. RELIANCE

There are two types of reliance damages that a party can incur. The first type involves actions done in reliance upon a valid and binding contract that is subsequently breached. In either case, the goal of the court is to put the nonbreaching party in as favorable a position as he enjoyed prior to the contract. Reliance damages are usually awarded if expectation damages are too uncertain. The second type involves the doctrine of promissory estoppel and results when there is no valid contract, but a party detrimentally relied on another's promise and it is unfair not to enforce the promise (Rest. 2d. § 90).

A. Requirements

Mnemonic: **Robin hood Finds Danger Inviting**

To recover for reliance a party must show:

1. That there was actual **R**eliance on the contract or promise,

2. That the reliance was **F**oreseeable to the breaching party,

3. That it was clearly **D**etrimental, and

4. That **I**njustice can only be avoided by enforcement.

B. Reliance upon a Contract (Rest. 2d. § 349)

1. Types of Reliance Damages

    a. Expenses Incurred in Preparation of Performance
    These are not part of the contract but are necessary to perform it.

    b. Expenditures Made in Performance Prior to Breach

    c. Foregone Opportunities
    Sometimes a court will grant the value of wages a party would have received had he remained at a prior job and not entered into the contract.

2. Limitations on reliance damages:

    a. Net Loss
    If full performance by the breaching party would have resulted in a net loss to the nonbreaching party, the amount of the loss is deducted from the reliance damages award.

    b. Foreseeability and Certainty
    Reliance damages must be foreseeable to the breaching party and must be proved with certainty.

c. Mitigation
The nonbreaching party has an obligation to mitigate his damages, if possible.

d. Cost to Plaintiff
The amount of reliance damages is determined by the costs incurred, regardless of the value of the benefit the breaching party received.

e. Essential v. Incidental Reliance Damages
Under the classical view, reliance damages were limited to a maximum of the full contract price. In such cases, a party could recover only essential reliance damages, i.e., expenses made in preparation for or in actual performance of the contract. The modern view allows recovery beyond the contract price in cases where incidental reliance naturally and foreseeably follows from the contract. Incidental expenses are those made in reliance upon having a contract, although they are not actually incurred in preparation or performance of the contract. Example: A rents a store from B for $100 and buys inventory worth $500. B breaks the lease before A takes possession. A can recover (1) rent paid to date ($100) in performance of the contract and (2) unsold inventory purchased in reliance on the lease (incidental).

C. Promissory Estoppel (Rest. 2d. § 90)
Promissory estoppel is an equitable doctrine that is used to avoid injustice by enforcing otherwise unenforceable promises. It "estops" the promisor from claiming that no consideration was given.
Exemplary Situations:

1. Promise to Make Gift
A promises to pay B, his son, $1,000 a week for life. B quits his job in reliance on the promise. A cannot revoke the offer if it would cause injustice, such as if B is unable to obtain new employment.

2. Charitable Subscriptions
Promises to make donations are enforceable absent consideration, even if there is no detrimental reliance.

3. Bids by Subcontractors (Rest. 2d. § 87)
A subcontractor who submits a "sub-bid" to a general contractor for use in computing the general contract bid must give the contractor a reasonable amount of time to accept, even if no consideration is given to keep the offer (bid) open.

IV. RESTITUTION

A court may require the breaching party to disgorge the value of any benefits received from the nonbreaching party. Unlike reliance damages, restitution is based upon the value of the benefit to the defendant rather than the cost to plaintiff. Restitution is granted when expectation damages are uncertain and reliance damages do not properly reflect the value defendant has received. The main goal of such damages is to avoid unjust enrichment. (Rest. 2d. § 370.)

A. Value of Benefit to Defendant (Rest. 2d. § 371)

The value of the benefit a party has received is measured in one of two ways:

1. The reasonable value of such a "benefit" as measured by the market value of obtaining it from another source (not the subjective value to the defendant).

2. The extent to which the party's property has increased in value or other interests have been advanced where the benefit is not readily obtainable from another source.

B. Limits on Restitution

1. Restitution can exceed the contract price if defendant was actually "enriched" beyond that amount.

2. If plaintiff has completed performance, then expectation damages are given and restitution is not available.

C. Recovery in Quasi-contract
Recovery in quasi-contract occurs in one of three general situations: (1) if a contract never existed but justice requires that the plaintiff be compensated; (2) if there was an unenforceable contract (due to the Statute of Frauds, illegality, etc.); and (3) if the plaintiff has materially breached an existing, valid contract and has conferred a benefit on the other party. Courts generally award either restitution or reliance damages, depending on fairness and equity.

1. Requirements of Quasi-contract:

    a. One party provided a benefit to another.

    b. The benefit was provided with the "reasonable expectation" of compensation.

    c. There was an express or implied request for the benefit.

    d. Party receiving the benefit would be unjustly enriched if he was not forced to compensate the party providing the benefits.

2. The size of recovery in quasi-contract (also called *quantum meruit*) is determined by the degree of the plaintiff's detriment.

3. If a party willfully breaches a contract, it is less likely that a court will grant quasi-contractual recovery, although this restriction is somewhat eased in cases of employment contracts in which an employee intentionally breaches.

4. UCC § 2-718
A breaching buyer may recover the value of payments made to the seller before the breach that exceed any liquidated damages clause or, if there is no such clause, the value of

such payments in excess of 20 percent of the contract price or $500, whichever is less. The seller can offset such recovery by any damages suffered.

CASE CLIPS

Laredo Hides Co. v. H & H Meat Products Co. (1974)

Facts: H & H breached a contract to sell cattle hides to Laredo. Laredo purchased hides on the open market and sued for the difference in prices.

Issue: If the seller breaches, is a buyer entitled to recover the difference between the cost of "cover" and the contract price?

Rule: When a seller wrongfully breaches a contract, the buyer can "cover" by purchasing the goods elsewhere in good faith and recover the difference between the price of the substituted goods and the contract price. (UCC § 2-712.)

Note: The buyer is also entitled to incidental and consequential damages.

Sullivan v. O'Connor (1973)

Facts: Sullivan sued her surgeon for breach of contract after the plastic surgery he performed on her nose failed to "enhance her beauty and improve her appearance" as expressly promised.

Issue: Does a doctor breach a contract if a medical procedure does not produce the desired results?

Rule: If a doctor expressly promises that a procedure will produce certain results, a patient may recover damages if that promise is not fulfilled.

Note: Because of the fear that patients will elevate a doctor's opinion to a promise, some courts require written proof of the promise. Other courts completely deny recovery in such cases.

White v. Benkowski (1967)

Facts: The Whites contracted to receive water from the well of their neighbors, the Benkowskis. The Benkowskis maliciously shut off the water supply for short periods of time after the initially friendly relationship of the parties deteriorated. The Whites sought compensatory and punitive damages.

Issue 1: May a court reduce a jury award for compensatory damages in the belief that such damages were not adequately proven?
Rule 1: Compensatory damages need not be proven with precision; evidence of damages shall be reviewed in the light most favorable to the plaintiff.
Issue 2: Are punitive damages awarded for a breach of contract?
Rule 2: Punitive damages are not available in breach of contract actions.

McCallister v. Patton (1948)

Facts: McCallister, a used car dealer, gave Patton, a new car dealer, a deposit on a new car. Patton refused to perform and returned the deposit when he discovered McCallister's occupation. New cars were difficult to obtain at that time.
Issue: When may a buyer obtain specific performance of a sales contract?
Rule: Specific performance of a sales contract is allowed only when damages will not suffice because the item was unique or of sentimental value. Mere scarcity does not establish uniqueness.

Laclede Gas Co. v. Amoco Oil Co. (1975)

Facts: Amoco breached a long-term contract to supply Laclede with propane. Although alternative suppliers of the gas were readily available, none were willing to enter into a long-term contract because of uncertainty as to future energy supplies and prices.
Issue: Can a sales contract be specifically enforced if there is no adequate alternative remedy at law?
Rule: Specific performance is granted if a remedy at law is inadequate because such remedy is not as certain, prompt, complete, and efficient to attain the ends of justice as is specific performance.

Northern Delaware Indus. Dev. Co. v. E.W. Bliss Co. (1986) Note Case

Facts: A clause in Bliss's contract to refurbish Northern Delaware's steel plant provided that Bliss should hire additional workers on night shift during certain parts of the work. Northern Delaware sought enforcement of the clause after Bliss fell behind schedule.
Issue: Will a court grant specific performance of a complicated construction contract?

Rule: Specific enforcement of large and complicated construction contracts is generally denied on the grounds that it would be impracticable to effectively enforce such an order.

Hamer v. Sidway (1891)

Facts: A young man's uncle promised to pay him $5,000 if he abstained from drinking, smoking, swearing and gambling until the age of 21. The uncle's executor refused to honor the promise, claiming that no consideration was given to the uncle in exchange for his promise.

Issue: Does voluntary forbearance of a legal right constitute consideration?

Rule: Forbearance of a right is a sufficient legal detriment to satisfy the requirement of consideration.

Fiege v. Boehm (1956)

Facts: Fiege agreed to pay medical and other expenses of Boehm provided that Boehm would not institute a paternity suit. After Boehm gave birth, Fiege used blood tests to prove he was not the father. He then refused to honor his promise, claiming absence of valid consideration.

Issue: Does forbearance to bring suit qualify as consideration if the suit would not have been successful?

Rule: Forbearance to assert an invalid claim is sufficient consideration if the forbearing party had an honest intention to prosecute the litigation and reasonably believed it was valid.

State ex rel. Ludwick v. Bryant (1985) Note Case

Facts: Bryant's corporation declared bankruptcy and ceased operations. Shortly thereafter, the Kansas Department of Human Resources told her that she was liable for one of her corporation's outstanding debts. In return for a personal guarantee to pay the debt in several monthly installments, Human Resources agreed not to sue the corporation. Bryant refused to make the payments, and Human Resources sued.

Issue: Is an agreement to refrain from asserting an unenforceable claim valid consideration?

Rule: Forbearance to assert an unenforceable claim is valueless, and thus not valid consideration.

Feinberg v. Pfeiffer Co. (1959)

Facts: Pfeiffer agreed to pay Feinberg $200 per month for life when she retired. She worked for a few more years and retired at the age of fifty-seven. Several years later, her pension was terminated when she refused to accept only $100 per month.

Issue 1: Do past services constitute valid consideration?

Rule 1: Past services are not valid consideration for a contract.

Issue 2: Does retirement in response to promise of an annuity constitute adequate consideration for enforcement of that promise?

Rule 2: Retirement from a lucrative position in response to the promise of a pension constitutes detrimental reliance and will warrant enforcement of the promise if injustice would otherwise result.

Kirksey v. Kirksey (1845)

Facts: The defendant wrote to his sister-in-law, "If you will come down and see me, I will let you have a place to raise your family." Two years after her relocation, he changed his mind and made her leave. The plaintiff claims that the expenses she incurred in moving were valid consideration.

Issue: Is an act necessary to accept a promise simply a precondition to a gratuitous act or consideration given in exchange for the promise?

Rule: Acts that are required before fulfillment of a promise are preconditions to accepting the promise, not valid consideration.

Note: A famous example of this rule involved a man who told another, "If you go to the shop around the corner, you can buy a coat on my credit." The walk around the corner is a precondition to accepting the promise. It was not done "in exchange" for the coat.

Central Adjustment Bureau, Inc. v. Ingram (1984)

Facts: After being hired at CAB, a collection agency, Ingram and two colleagues were made to sign noncompetition agreements if they wished to continue working there. Several years later, they resigned and formed a competing collection agency with CAB's client lists, claiming that the noncompetition agreement was void for lack of consideration.

Issue: Is a noncompetition agreement invalid for failure of consideration if it was signed after at-will employment had begun?

Rule: Continued employment constitutes valid consideration for a noncompetition agreement signed after at-will employment has begun.
Note: Despite this rule, courts are generally hostile to noncompetition agreements which are not sufficiently limited in scope of location and time.

Strong v. Sheffield (1895)

Facts: Sheffield guaranteed her husband's debt to Strong on the condition that he would forbear from demanding payment for an unspecified period of time. Strong forbore for two years before presenting the note for collection. Sheffield claimed her guarantee was unenforceable for lack of consideration, because Strong's promise was illusory. Payment could have been demanded at any time without violating the letter of his promise to ask for the money when he wanted it.
Issue: Does a promise to forbear collection of a debt for an unspecified period of time constitute valid consideration?
Rule: Forbearance to collect on a note is illusory and insufficient consideration if the forbearer had the option of demanding payment at any time.

Mattei v. Hopper (1958)

Facts: Mattei agreed to buy Hopper's shopping center. The agreement called for a $1,000 down payment and the balance to be paid within 120 days subject to Mattei obtaining satisfactory leases. Hopper refused to complete the sale, claiming Mattei's promise was illusory because he was not actually bound: Hopper was obligated to sell, but Mattei only had to buy if he was satisfied with the leases.
Issue: Does a contract lack consideration if the assent of one party to the agreement is conditioned by a satisfaction clause?
Rule: An agreement that contains a satisfaction clause is not illusory (lacking consideration or mutuality of obligation) if performance of the condition can be judged by a reasonable person standard or if the party subject to the satisfaction clause acts in good faith.

Eastern Airlines v. Gulf Oil Corp. (1975)

Facts: Gulf contracted to fulfill Eastern's jet fuel requirements on a long-term basis. The parties agreed that price would be determined by an index of posted fuel prices. In 1974 when oil prices skyrocketed as

a result of an OPEC embargo of foreign fuel sources, posted prices were kept below the market level by government regulation. Gulf refused to perform, claiming that there was no mutuality because Eastern was not obligated to buy a set amount.
Issue: Are requirements contracts void for lack of mutuality?
Rule: Requirements contracts, entered into in good faith, are not void for lack of mutuality. According to UCC § 2-306, such contracts are valid so long as the requirements are not varied in bad faith or grossly disproportionate to a reasonably foreseeable figure.

Wood v. Lucy, Lady Duff-Gordon (1917)

Facts: Lady Duff-Gordon, a famous designer, agreed with Wood that he would have exclusive agency to place her endorsements on clothing designs, to place her designs on sale and to license others to market them. In exchange, Wood promised to keep the books and to split the profits evenly with Duff-Gordon. Duff-Gordon breached by endorsing designs herself and keeping the profits. In defense, she claimed that Wood's promise was illusory, as she had granted him exclusive agency, but he was not obligated to find designs or to sell her labels.
Issue: Is a contract void for lack of mutuality because one party did not promise to use reasonable efforts to perform his duties?
Rule: A promise to use reasonable efforts can be implied from a contract and, therefore, a contract does not fail for lack of mutuality because it does not contain explicit clauses requiring good faith efforts (UCC § 2-306(2)).

Ricketts v. Scothorn (1898)

Facts: Ricketts signed a note promising his granddaughter $2,000 on demand so that she would not have to work. She quit her job in reliance on the promise. The administrator of Ricketts' estate refused to honor the note after Ricketts' death, claiming that no consideration was given for his promise.
Issue: When will a gratuitous promise bind a promisor?
Rule: The doctrine of equitable estoppel provides that a right may accrue to a promisee if the promisee changed her position in accordance with the real or apparent intention of the promisor.

East Providence Credit Union v. Geremia (1968)

Facts: The Geremias secured a loan from East Providence by using their car as collateral. The loan agreement provided that if the Geremias' insurance lapsed, East Providence could make the payments and add the amount to the balance owed. On one occasion, the Geremias agreed that East Providence should pay the premium, which it failed to do. The uninsured car was destroyed in an accident.

Issue: May the doctrine of estoppel be applied to promises to act in the future?

Rule: The doctrine of promissory estoppel, expressed in Restatement § 90, provides that a promise to act in the future, which the promisor should reasonably expect to induce reliance, will be enforced, if the promise induced reliance and injustice can only be avoided by enforcement of the promise.

Callano v. Oakwood Park Homes Corp. (1966)

Facts: Pendergast contracted with Oakwood to buy a house and with Callano to plant shrubs on the lot. Upon Pendergast's death, Callano had not been paid, and the sales contract with Oakwood was voided. Oakwood sold the property, enhanced by the shrubs, to another buyer. Callano sued Oakwood for unjust enrichment.

Issue: Is there quasi-contractual liability for services or goods received from a party with whom the receiver did not have a direct relationship?

Rule: Recovery based on quasi-contract is only allowed when a direct relationship exists between the parties or there is a mistake on the part of the party conferring the benefit.

Cotnam v. Wisdom (1907)

Facts: Wisdom and another doctor rendered care unsuccessfully to Cotnam's decedent after the decedent was thrown from a streetcar. Wisdom sued to recover the value of the services he rendered.

Issue 1: May a doctor recover for the value of services rendered when no express contract was made with the patient?

Rule 1: A doctor may recover under the theory of quasi-contract for the reasonable value of services provided during an emergency.

Issue 2: What amount can a doctor recover for emergency services provided under quasi-contract?

Rule 2: The value of emergency services rendered by a doctor should be determined according to the time, service and skill employed. The financial standing of the victim is not relevant.
Note: There is no question that a contract in the formal sense does not exist, because the unconscious victim could never have made an "offer" to the doctor. However, courts will sometimes impose an obligation to pay in order to encourage people to help one another.

Mills v. Wyman (1825)

Facts: Mills provided board, nursing, and care to Wyman's 25-year-old-son who became ill while traveling. After the services had been rendered, Wyman wrote to Mills, promising to pay for them. Wyman later refused to pay.
Issue: Is moral obligation sufficient consideration to support a promise?
Rule: Moral obligation is not sufficient consideration to enforce a promise to pay for services already rendered. Past consideration is no consideration.

Webb v. McGowin (1935)

Facts: Webb was crippled in the course of a heroic act to prevent harm to McGowin. Consequently, McGowin promised Webb $15 every two weeks for the rest of Webb's life. McGowin made payments until his death, whereupon his estate refused to honor the promise.
Issue: When is moral obligation sufficient consideration to enforce a promise?
Rule: Moral obligation is sufficient consideration to support a subsequent promise when the promisor received a material benefit.
Note: This is the minority rule. The majority view is that moral obligation is no consideration. (See *Mills v. Wyman.*)

Chapter 2

THE BARGAINING PROCESS

To create a valid contract, three general requirements must be met.

Mnemonic: **Mother Adores Cigars After Dinner**

(1) Mutual Assent
(2) Consideration
(3) Absence of Defenses

This chapter primarily deals with mutual assent, also called a "meeting of the minds". It embodies the idea that all parties should have a similar understanding of the contract they agree to enter. To achieve mutual assent, the parties often undergo a negotiated process whereby each makes proposals and counterproposals until they arrive at a mutually acceptable arrangement. The process ends when one side *accepts* the other side's *offer* (proposal).

I. OFFER

An offer is a manifestation of willingness to enter into a bargain which invites another person's assent to the bargain which assent will, in turn, conclude the arrangement (Rest. 2d. § 24). One who makes an offer is the offeror, and the person to whom it is made is the offeree. To be a valid offer (i.e., to constitute an offer), a manifestation of intent to enter a bargain must have "the 3 C's":

Commitment or promise by the offeror to enter into a contract
Certainty and definitiveness of essential terms
Communication by offeror to offeree

A. Commitment or Promise

The first requirement for an offer is that it embody a promise or commitment, as opposed to a statement of present intention or preliminary negotiation. Statements such as "I intend to sell you my car" or "come talk to me about buying my car" are not offers. Saying "if you pay me $100, I will sell you my car" is a valid offer.

1. Objective Test

   Whether a statement is an offer depends on whether a reasonable person would so understand it, regardless of the parties' subjective understanding. For example, given the trade customs of an industry, would a reasonable person think that an offer was made? The courts consider several factors:

   Mnemonic: **LIMPS**

   a. Language

      Have the words "offer" or "promise" been used? Courts also consider the definitiveness of the terms and language of a proposal to help decide whether it is an offer. "First come, first served" may indicate an offer because it provides buyers with a clear means of accepting by buying first.

   b. Industry Customs

      Courts determine whether the type of language and manner of the proposal is usually considered to be an offer in a specific industry.

   c. Method of Communication

      Communications made by mass media (i.e., TV, newspaper, billboard) are often held to be invitations for offers, not actual offers. For example, a TV ad announces that a dealer has 100 cars for sale for $1000 each. The dealer did not make an offer to the entire TV audience (which could be millions) to buy his cars for $1000. Rather, he "invited" members of the audience to offer to buy his cars.

d. Prior Practices Between the Parties
If the parties had prior transactions, the courts will consider the significance of the questioned statements in light of statements made in previous dealings.

e. Surrounding Circumstances
Courts also consider the manner and context in which a statement was made (e.g., in jest, with anger, etc.), and whether it was reasonable to construe the statement as an offer under those circumstances.

2. Commitments/promises are distinguished from opinions.
A hired B to pick A's crops, partly because B told A that the task would take approximately two or three weeks. B has not made an offer to pick the crop in two to three weeks, unless he actually guaranteed that he could do it in that time.

3. Price Quotations
A price quotation is not an offer to sell unless:

a. The quoter specifies the quantity he is willing to sell, not merely the per-unit cost, and

b. The quote is made to a specific person, not the general public.

4. Auctions
An auctioneer solicits bids; he does not make offers.

B. Certainty of Terms
The subject matter of a proposal must be definite and certain; otherwise, a court would be unable to determine the terms if the offer evolves into an enforceable contract. The consequences of missing or vague terms are as follows:

1. Time of Payment and Performance
The absence of these terms is not fatal because the court can imply that performance is due within a reasonable time. (UCC § 2-309.)

2. Identity of the parties and subject matter
   These must be certain.

3. Quantity Must be Specified
   Quantity is a required term except for output and requirement contracts (see below). An employment contract that has no specific duration is considered to be terminable at will.

4. Price
   Price and other missing terms can be implied. (UCC § 2-305.) However, if the parties clearly show the absence of agreement on price, price will not be implied and there will be no contract.

5. Part Performance or Acceptance
   Vagueness and uncertainty of terms can also be overcome if there is part performance or acceptance.

   a. Part Performance
      If the parties have already begun performing the contract, the manner in which they acted upon vague terms can be determinative of their meaning.

   b. Acceptance
      If the contract terms are uncertain, acceptance of one possible interpretation will establish the terms.

   c. Terms to be Agreed Upon
      Offers that include some of the terms and state that other terms will be agreed upon in the future are too vague if the omitted terms are material to the agreement (e.g., quantity), and a contract will not be formed even if this "offer" is "accepted."

6. Output and Requirements Contracts
   Output and requirements contracts are valid despite an absence of definite terms, so long as both parties act in good faith.

   a. Requirements Contract
      Airline contracts with Refinery to supply it with "all the jet fuel it needs." There is no definite quantity, but if Airline makes a good-faith effort to buy a certain amount of fuel and Refinery makes a good-faith effort to provide it, the contract is valid.

   b. Output Contract
      A cereal company contracts with Farmer to buy "all wheat grown in year X." Neither knows how much wheat will be sold, but the absence of a specific quantity is not fatal in such a situation.

C. Communication to the Offeree
The offeree must have knowledge of the offer.

II. TERMINATION OF AN OFFER

Once an offer is made the power of acceptance is created in the offeree; if he accepts the offer, the offeror must perform. Termination of the offer extinguishes this power. An offer can only be terminated before the offeree accepts it. Termination can occur by an act of either party or by operation of law.

A. Revocation by the Offeror
An offeror can revoke his offer so long as it has not been accepted by the offeree. An offer can be terminated in various ways:

1. Communication to the Offeree
   Communication of termination of an offer can be direct or indirect. Indirect communication may involve a third party who notifies the offeree of the offeror's revocation. The indirect communication must be correct, given by a reliable

source, and be understood by a "reasonable person." Example: A makes an offer to B then sells the item to C before B accepts. The act of selling to another is a reasonable indication of revocation if B is aware of the sale. However, if B is not *notified* of A's revocation – either directly or indirectly – before he accepts, then the acceptance is valid and A must sell to B.

2. By Publication
   Offers that are made by publication can be revoked by publication. Unlike direct and indirect communications, the revocation is effective when published, not when it is received by the offeree.

B. Irrevocable Offers

An offeror can generally terminate his offer, even if he promised not to do so. However, offers cannot be revoked under certain circumstances.

Mnemonic: **DROP FU**

1. Detrimental Reliance
   Offers are irrevocable for a reasonable time period if the offeree relied to his detriment on the offer being held open, and it is reasonably foreseeable to the offeror that the offeree would so rely. Example: A general contractor relies on a sub-contractor's offer in determining the costs of the overall job.

2. Options
   If the offeree gave consideration for the promise that the offer would be kept open, it must be. It is, in essence, a contract to contract. Example: A gives B $20 not to revoke his promise for two weeks. Section 87 of the Restatement (Second) holds an option contract valid even if there is no actual consideration, so long as consideration is recited in a written and signed document.

3. Partial Performance of a Unilateral Contract
   Traditionally, a unilateral contract was revocable at any time prior to completion of the requested performance. For example, A promises to pay B $100 if B crosses a bridge. B "accepts" only by crossing the bridge. A can revoke at any time before B reaches the other side. Today, the majority and Restatement Second view is that a contract is formed when performance begins (i.e., when B starts crossing), provided that it is completed within a reasonable time. The offeror cannot revoke, but the offeree can discontinue his performance at any time. However, preparation to begin performance is not considered to be partial performance (e.g., when B puts on his bridge-crossing shoes and says his pre-crossing mantra).

4. Firm Offers (UCC § 2-205)
   A signed writing by a merchant to buy or sell goods that has firm terms and assures that the offer will be held open is enforceable, even without consideration. Duration:

   a. Period stated
      If the period is actually stated, the offer will remain open for the stated period or three months, whichever is less.

   b. Period not stated
      If the period is not stated, the offer remains open for a "reasonable time," not to exceed three months.

C. Termination by the Offeree
An offeree can terminate an offer in three ways:

1. Express rejection

2. Counteroffer
   A counteroffer occurs when an offeree tries to add or change terms in the original offer. This is considered a rejection of the original offer, as well as a new offer. Example: A offers to sell his car to B. B makes a counteroffer to buy the car if A repaints it. A's original offer to sell has been rejected, and

B's offer to buy with additional conditions is the new offer. A is actually the offeree now.

a. Mere Inquiry
A "mere inquiry" is not a counteroffer. As long as offeree suggests that he is still considering the original offer, a counteroffer has not been made. Example: B tells A, "I'm still thinking about buying your car, but I would like to know how you feel about lowering the price."

b. Irrevocable Offer
A counteroffer does not revoke an irrevocable offer.

c. Date Effective
A rejection is effective when it is received by the offeror, who then can extend a new offer to another party.

d. Battle-of-the-forms Exception
See Acceptance, below.

3. Passage of time
If an offer specifies a time within which it must be accepted, failure to accept within that time period will constitute a rejection. If no time period is specified, a reasonable time period is given for response. In either case, the time period starts when the offeree actually gets the offer.

D. Termination by Law

1. Death or incapacity
The death or incapacity (e.g., insanity) of either party before the offer is accepted will terminate the offer. The death or incapacity does not have to be communicated to the other party. Irrevocable offers are not terminated by death or incapacity. (Rest. 2d. § 48.)

2. If the subject of the offer, such as the goods offered for sale, is destroyed prior to acceptance, the offer is terminated. (Rest. 2d. § 35.)

3. If the contract becomes contrary to law prior to acceptance, the offer will be terminated. (Rest. 2d. § 35.) Example: A offers to sell liquor to B. While the offer is open, Congress outlaws alcohol consumption. A's offer is terminated. Had B already accepted, the contract would become void.

III. ACCEPTANCE

An acceptance is a manifestation of assent to the terms of an offer in the manner required by the offer. A contract is created once an acceptance is communicated. To be valid an acceptance must meet the following requirements:

A. Acceptor

Only the specific person to whom the offer was made can accept. The power of acceptance cannot be assigned. Exception: an option can be assigned.

B. Communication

Acceptance of an offer for a bilateral contract is not effective until it is communicated to the offeror.

1. Objective Manifestation of Assent Required
The offeree's subjective state of mind is irrelevant. However, the offeree must realize that an offer was made. Absent such knowledge, his acceptance is invalid.

2. Acceptance Received by the Offeror
The obvious situation is where the offeree conveys acceptance to the offeror, either by telephone communication or in person. But problems can develop if there is a delay between the time the offeree accepts and the time the offeror receives the communication, such as when the offeree accepts by mail.

   a. Mailbox Rule (majority)
   An acceptance is effective (and a contract is thus formed) upon the dispatch, not the actual receipt, of the accep-

tance. Exceptions:

i. The offer explicitly states that acceptance is not effective until actually received.

ii. Options
Exercise (i.e., acceptance) of an option contract is only effective upon receipt by the offeror.

b. An offeror can specify the means of acceptance of his offer (e.g., only upon actual receipt or in a specified place).

c. If offeror does not specify the method of conveying acceptance then any reasonable means is valid. Even if a specific method is given, an acceptance that is conveyed in a different way is valid if it is actually received by the offeror before he revokes the offer.

d. Acceptance Lost in Transmission
An acceptance that is lost in transmission is valid if it was properly sent, but may be excused if it will cause hardship to the offeror, such as if offeror already sold the property.

e. Restatement (Second) § 40 Exception
In general, a rejection becomes effective upon receipt and an offer is effective upon dispatch. However, where an offeree dispatches a rejection and then dispatches an acceptance, the acceptance is only effective if received before the rejection. Examples:

i. Rejection Before Acceptance
An offeree mails a rejection on Monday and an acceptance on Tuesday. Both letters are delivered on Wednesday. The acceptance is effective only if the offeror gets it before he receives the rejection.

ii. Acceptance Before Rejection
Offeree mails acceptance on Monday and it is delivered on Thursday. Offeree also mails a rejection on Tuesday and it arrives on Wednesday.

(1) Majority Rule
Under the mailbox rule, acceptance is effective as of Monday unless the offeror limited the manner of conveying the acceptance. However, the offeror may be able to prevent the contract under the theory of estoppel by showing that he relied on the rejection to his detriment.

(2) Minority Rule
Some courts rule that if an offeror actually receives the rejection first, no contract can be created.

f. "Crossing" Communications
If two parties send identical offers to each other, neither one knowing of the other's offer, a contract is not formed when the offers "cross in the mail." There must be knowledge of an offer before a contract can be formed.

g. Mistake in Transmission
If an offer is mistakenly changed *during* the process of transmission to the offeree (e.g., teletype or clerical error) and the offeree does not know and could not reasonably have been expected to know of the error, then the offer can be accepted on its mistaken terms (majority view).

3. Exceptions to the Requirement of Communication of Acceptance

Mnemonic: **Search And Will Destroy**

a. Silence
If an offeree does not respond to an offer but accepts the benefits of the offer, and prior dealings or custom would

lead a reasonable person to believe that this is the way in which an acceptance is made, then silence can constitute acceptance.

b. Act
If an offeror specifies that performance of a certain act will constitute acceptance, performing the requisite act will form a contract. Note: This is not a unilateral contract – an act in return for a promise; rather, the act here is used to symbolize the promise.

c. Waiver Expressly Contained in the Offer
The offeror may expressly waive communication of acceptance.

d. Dominion
In general, if an "offeree" accepts unsolicited goods and exercises dominion over them, he has accepted an offer (to purchase the goods) and formed a contract. However, some states have statutes that classify unsolicited goods as gifts to the recipient.

4. Unilateral Contracts
In the context of unilateral contracts, performance of an act (as opposed to making a promise for bilateral contracts) constitutes acceptance of the offer. The offeree's act must be consummated:

a. With the knowledge of the offeror and motivation from the offer.

b. Completely.
The offeree must completely perform the requisite act. Partial performance merely creates an option for the offeree to complete the performance and form a contract.

c. With notification to the offeror (majority rule).

The offeree must notify the offeror, even after completing performance, if the offeree's performance would not otherwise come to the offeror's attention.

C. Variations from Offer's Terms

Variations from the terms of the offer do not necessarily invalidate an acceptance.

1. Common Law View

Any variation in the acceptance constitutes a rejection of the offer and an extension of a counteroffer. This was sometimes called the "last shot rule" because contracting parties often varied their acceptances in an effort to get the "last shot"; that is, by sending a counteroffer instead of an acceptance, each side would try to manipulate the terms of the final agreement to its favor.

2. UCC § 2-207

A written acceptance of an offer for the "sale of goods" is valid, notwithstanding terms that vary from the offer, unless acceptance is expressly conditioned on assent to the additional or different terms. This has been referred to as the "first shot rule": there is some incentive to send out the first form, against which the consistency of future terms is to be judged.

3. Battle of the Forms and Related Problems

In routine business transactions, most parties use standardized printed forms. However, one company's standard forms rarely match the other's. A "battle of the forms" results when courts have to decide whose forms govern.

a. Conditional Acceptance

If a party sends an acceptance that is conditional upon the offeror's assent to new or conflicting terms that are included in the acceptance, there is no contract until and unless the original offeror manifests his acceptance.

b. Acceptance Contains Additional Terms

i. Neither party is a merchant –
The contract terms are those of the original offer.

ii. One party is not a merchant –
The additional terms become part of the contract if the offeror explicitly assents.

iii. All parties are merchants –
The additional term becomes part of the contract unless the offeror objects or the term is a material alteration.

c. Offer and Acceptance Differ on a Particular Issue (varying but not additional terms)

i. Knockout Rule (majority)
The disputed terms are "knocked out" of both the offer and acceptance, and UCC standard "gap fillers" (e.g., implied time of performance) control.

ii. Minority Rule
Offeror's clause overrides ("first shot").

d. Written Confirmation of Oral Agreement

i. Under UCC § 2-207, additional terms contained in a written confirmation are treated the same as additional terms contained in an acceptance (see above).

ii. When the confirmation contains terms that differ from the oral agreement, the terms of the oral agreement usually control.

e. If an acceptance materially deviates from the offer, it will not be effective.

i. Material deviations usually involve price, quality, quantity, or delivery terms.

ii. Although the writings of the parties do not establish a contract, conduct by both parties recognizing the existence of a contract is sufficient to establish a contract. The terms consist of those terms on which the writings agree, together with gap fillers from the UCC. (UCC § 2-207(3).)

f. If the parties use custom-written offer and acceptance forms, as opposed to standardized contract forms, then the traditional offer and acceptance rules apply without variation.

CASE CLIPS

Lucy v. Zehmer (1954)

Facts: Zehmer signed a memorandum agreeing to sell his family farm to Lucy. Zehmer claimed that it was part of a joke he was playing on Lucy.

Issue: Can a contract be avoided if one party claims that the "whole matter was a joke?"

Rule: The intention of a party to a contract is judged by his words and acts (objective standard), not by his unexpressed state of mind (subjective standard).

Sullivan v. O'Connor (1973)

Facts: Sullivan sued her surgeon for breach of contract after the plastic surgery performed on her nose failed to "enhance her beauty and improve her appearance" as expressly promised.

Issue: Does a doctor breach a contract if a medical procedure does not produce the desired results?

Rule: If a doctor expressly promises that a procedure will produce certain results, a patient may recover damages if that promise is not fulfilled.

Note: Because of the fear that patients will elevate a doctor's opinion to a promise, some courts require written proof of the promise. Other courts completely deny recovery in such cases.

Owen v. Tunison (1932)

Facts: Owen wrote Tunison to ask if he would sell his store property for $6,000. Tunison replied "It would not be possible for me to sell it unless I received $16,000 cash." Owen then wrote back accepting this term but Tunison refused to sell.

Issue: Is a price quote in response to an inquiry an offer to sell?

Rule: A seller's minimum acceptable price is not an offer to sell, but rather an invitation to negotiate.

Harvey v. Facey (1893) Note Case

Facts: Harvey was interested in a piece of property owned by Facey. He sent Facey a telegram asking him the minimum price for which he would sell the property. Facey quoted a price and Harvey sent a telegram stating that he would pay it. Harvey sued for specific performance.

Issue: Does a statement of the minimum price at which a vendor will sell constitute an offer?

Rule: A mere statement of the lowest price at which a vendor will sell is not an offer to sell at that price to the person making the inquiry.

Fairmount Glass Works v. Crunden-Martin Woodenware Co. (1899)

Facts: Crunden-Martin asked Fairmount to quote the "lowest price" at which it would sell certain goods. Fairmount provided a price quote sheet with terms and conditions "for immediate acceptance." Crunden-Martin sent in an order, but Fairmount refused to fill it.

Issue: Is a price quote an offer if it includes the phrase "for immediate acceptance"?

Rule: Use of the phrase "for immediate acceptance" in a price quote has the legal effect of making the quote an offer.

Note: Price quotations are generally not considered offers, especially if they are unsolicited.

Craft v. Elder & Johnston Co. (1941)

Facts: The Elder & Johnston Company advertised a sewing machine for $26 as a "Thursday Only Special." It refused to sell the machine to Craft.
Issue: Is an advertisement an offer that a member of the public can accept?
Rule: An advertisement is not an offer. It is an invitation to negotiate and receive offers.

Lefkowitz v. Great Minneapolis Surplus Store, Inc. (1957) Note Case

Facts: The Great Minneapolis Surplus Store advertised in a newspaper that it would sell one valuable lapin stole for $1.00 on a "first come, first served" basis. Lefkowitz arrived first but the store would not sell him the lapin stole. It claimed the offer was for women only.
Issue: When is a newspaper advertisement considered an offer?
Rule: A newspaper advertisement that is clear, definite, explicit, and leaves nothing open for negotiation is considered to be an offer.

Elsinore Union Elementary Sch. Dist. v. Kastorff (1960)

Facts: Kastorff, a contractor, submitted an erroneous bid for work that was being contracted out by the school district. Kastorff had told the school district that the figures were correct because he did not know of the error. He notified the school district upon learning of the error, which was caused by a clerical mistake. The school district "accepted" the bid despite being informed of the error. Kastorff refused to do the work.
Issue: Is a party relieved of its obligation to perform because its offering price was erroneously calculated?
Rule: A party may be relieved of the obligation to perform according to its offer if the party to whom the offer was made knew, or had reason to know, of a material error in calculation of the price.
Note: Although courts grant relief for clerical errors, this is not the case with errors of judgment, i.e., if a contractor underestimates his costs.

International Filter Co. v. Conroe Gin, Ice & Light Co. (1925)

Facts: International Filter sold its products through traveling salesmen who carried order forms. The forms stated that a contract would be formed once a buyer "accepted" the offer by ordering the product, and an executive officer at International Filter's home office approved the order ("accepted" the acceptance). Conroe sent an order which was approved, but he later sought to cancel the order.
Issue: Must "acceptance of an acceptance" of an offer be directly and formally communicated?
Rule: A valid contract can be formed without communication of approval of acceptance if the offer indicates that such communication is not required.

White v. Corlies and Tift (1871)

Facts: White submitted an estimate to perform work for Corlies and Tift. Corlies and Tift then sent White an offer to do the work. White began work without formally communicating acceptance of the offer. Corlies and Tift changed its mind and revoked the offer.
Issue: Can an offer be accepted by beginning performance without giving any other indication of assent?
Rule: Acceptance of an offer must be actually communicated to the offeror.
Note: The resolution of this case turned on whether Corlies and Tift required return performance or a return promise in response. The court ruled that this was not a unilateral contract and therefore a return "promise" was required.

Ever-Tite Roofing Corp. v. Green (1955) Note Case

Facts: The Greens' offer to have Ever-Tite re-roof their house stated that acceptance could be given in writing or by commencing work. Since the entire job was to be done on credit, Ever-Tite had to verify the Greens' creditworthiness, which took eight days. Its workmen arrived to start work the next day and found that the Greens had hired another company (i.e., revoked the offer) two days earlier. They claimed that Ever-Tite waited too long to accept.
Issue: In the absence of an express provision, what is the time limit within which an offer must be accepted?

Rule: The power to create a contract by acceptance of an offer terminates at the time specified in the offer or, if no time is specified, at the end of a reasonable time. Where the offeror has reason to know of the delay in the offeree's acceptance (e.g., to get credit approval), it is reasonable to allot more time for acceptance.

Allied Steel and Conveyors, Inc.
v. Ford Motor Co. (1960)

Facts: Ford ordered machinery from Allied with its own order form which stated that the order was not binding until accepted and "acceptance should be executed on acknowledgment copy which should be returned to the buyer." A clause in the purchase order provided that Allied was to be liable for all injuries resulting from negligence in the installation of the machinery. It began installing the machinery without sending the acknowledgment copy as formal acceptance. An Allied employee was injured as a result of the negligence of Ford's employees in connection with Allied's work. Allied claimed it was not liable, because it did not formally accept the offer.
Issue: Can the beginning of performance act as an acceptance to an offer that provides a specific means of communicating acceptance?
Rule: Beginning performance with the knowledge, consent, and agreement of the offeror is a valid means of accepting an offer. "Acceptance should be executed on acknowledgment copy" is merely a suggestion.
Note: Although this case seems to contradict *White v. Corlies and Tift*, both courts were actually determining whether the offeror knew of the acceptance.

Dickinson v. Dodds (1876)

Facts: On June 10, Dodds offered to sell Dickinson a parcel of land, promising to keep the offer open until June 12. On June 11, Dickinson learned that Dodds intended to sell the land to another person. That afternoon Dickinson left a note accepting the offer.
Issue: What is the effect of an offer when the offeree has received notice that the offeror has made another offer that precludes the first offer?
Rule: Information that leads an offeree to reasonably conclude that an offer has been withdrawn voids the offer.

Minneapolis & St. Louis Ry. Co. v. Columbus Rolling-Mill Co. (1886)

Facts: In response to a query, Columbus provided the Minneapolis & St. Louis Railroad with a price quote for the purchase of 2,000 to 5,000 tons of iron rails. The railroad was given 12 days to accept. It ordered only 1,200 tons at the quoted price, and Columbus refused to fill the order. Before the 12 days were up, the railroad made a second order for 2,000 tons and Columbus again refused.
Issue: Is an "acceptance" that changes the terms of the offer, such as quantity, a rejection of the offer and a counteroffer?
Rule: Responding to an offer with an "acceptance" that changes a material term has the legal effect of being a rejection of the offer and is a counteroffer. The original offeror now has the power to reject or accept.

Dorton v. Collins & Aikman Corp. (1972)

Facts: The Carpet Mart made an oral offer to Collins & Aikman to buy carpeting. Collins & Aikman sent its standard acceptance form, which included an arbitration clause to settle disputes. When a dispute arose, it sought to settle by arbitration. The lower court ruled that since the acceptance included new terms, a contract was formed by the conduct of the parties and inconsistent terms should be "knocked out" as per UCC § 2-207.
Issue: Are parties bound by an arbitration clause included on the back of an acceptance form?
Rule: Under the "battle of the forms" rule of UCC § 2-207, a document can be an acceptance even if it is not a "mirror image" of the offer, provided that the conflicting term is not a material alteration.
Note: Some courts hold arbitration clauses to be material alterations.

St. Paul Structural Steel Co. v. ABI Contracting, Inc. (1985)

Facts: ABI made an offer to buy steel from St. Paul that included a clause permitting it to withhold 10 percent of the purchase price until completion of its construction project. St. Paul sent an acceptance that expressly excluded the clause.
Issue: Is a term of an offer voided by a confirmation that specifically states that term is void?

Rule: When an offer and acceptance contain conflicting nonmaterial terms, these terms will cancel each other out (UCC §2-207). The contract will consist of the terms upon which both parties have expressly agreed together with UCC "gap fillers."
Note: If a material term is disputed, the entire contract can be voided.

C. Itoh & Co. (America) Inc. v. Jordan Int'l. Co. (1977) Note Case

Facts: Itoh sent Jordan a purchase order which it accepted, subject to conditions printed on the reverse of the acceptance. The reverse contained an arbitration clause, which Jordan sought to enforce when a dispute subsequently arose. Itoh was unaware of the provision.
Issue: Does performance of a defective agreement give rise to a contract?
Rule: Under UCC § 2-207, if two parties subsequently perform believing they had formed a contract even when they have not, their actions constitute a contract based only on the terms to which they had actually agreed.

Drennan v. Star Paving Co. (1958)

Facts: Drennan, a contractor, used a bid from Star Paving, a subcontractor, to calculate the costs of a larger bid it was submitting to a third party. After Drennan was awarded the job, Star Paving claimed that its "sub-bid" was erroneously low, and refused to work at that price. Although it had not formally accepted the offer, Drennan had relied on the price, as is customary in the construction industry. It sued to recover the difference between the original price and the amount paid to another subcontractor to do the work.
Issue: May a party be required to perform by the terms of an offer that was never actually accepted?
Rule: If an offeror should reasonably expect that his offer will induce justifiable reliance by the offeree to take an action or forbearance of a substantial and definite character, the offer is enforceable even if the reliance occurs prior to a formal acceptance of the offer.

Holman Erection Co. v. Orville E. Madsen & Sons, Inc. (1983) Note Case

Facts: Madsen incorporated Holman's bid for a subcontract in its bid for a general contract. Madsen received the general contract but subcontracted with someone else instead of Holman.
Issue: Must a general contractor accept a subcontractor's offer if that subcontractor's offer is used in preparing an offer for a general contract that is later obtained?
Rule: The use of a subcontractor's bid in preparing the general bid does not constitute acceptance of the subcontractor's offer.

Grouse v. Group Health Plan, Inc. (1981)

Facts: Grouse resigned from his job because he received an employment offer from Group Health. The offer was later revoked.
Issue: Are damages resulting from revocation of an at-will employment offer recoverable?
Rule: Under the doctrine of promissory estoppel, a promise which the promisor should reasonably expect to induce action or forbearance on the part of the promisee, and which does induce such action, is binding if nonenforcement would result in injustice.

Hoffman v. Red Owl Stores (1965)

Facts: Relying on a representative of Red Owl's repeated advice and promises that he would be able to obtain a Red Owl supermarket franchise, Hoffman sold his existing business, moved to a new town, bought and sold a small grocery, and took out a loan. Red Owl later informed Hoffman that there would be no deal. Hoffman sued to recover lost income and expenses he incurred in reliance on Red Owl's promise. Red Owl claimed it was not liable because there was no contract, as it had never made Hoffman an offer.
Issue: Can a party be liable under the theory of promissory estoppel for breaking a promise, even though the terms of the promise were too vague and indefinite to constitute an offer?
Rule: A party will be liable for a promise made during preliminary negotiations if the promisor should reasonably expect to induce an action or forbearance of a definite and substantial nature by the promisee, the promise does induce such action or forbearance, and injustice would result if relief were not granted.

Channel Home Centers v. Grossman (1986)

Facts: Channel Home Centers and Grossman signed a letter of intent providing that they would negotiate in good faith for Channel to lease premises in a mall which was being purchased by Grossman, and that Grossman would withdraw the premises from the market. In return, Grossman used the letter to obtain credit. He later rented the premises to Channel Home's competitor.

Issue: Is a letter of intent in which the parties promise to bargain in good faith enforceable?

Rule: An agreement to negotiate in good faith is enforceable if the parties intended to be bound, there are definite terms, and there is consideration. In the instant case, the letter was enforceable because it was evidence of an intent to be bound, the terms were detailed in the letter, and the credit obtained by use of the letter was consideration.

Lee v. Joseph E. Seagram & Sons, Inc. (1977)

Facts: In return for an agreement to purchase Lee's liquor distributorship, Seagram orally promised to relocate Lee and his sons with a different distributorship in a different city. The Lees were never relocated. Seagram claimed that the promise was too vague and indefinite. However, Lee introduced evidence of the terms of the agreement, including the size and value of the new distributorship and industry methods and customs for evaluating distributorships. Furthermore, Lee provided evidence that the parties intended to bind themselves to the contract.

Issue: Is an agreement that lacks definite terms enforceable if there is an intent to contract and consideration passes?

Rule: A court can enforce a reasonably definite agreement when it is convinced that the parties intended to bind themselves to an enforceable agreement.

Chapter 3

STATUTE OF FRAUDS

The general rule in contracts is that most oral agreements are valid and enforceable. However, under the Statute of Frauds, which originated in England, certain types of contracts are only enforceable if they are in writing. The main purpose of the Statute is to prevent fraudulent claims by requiring that written evidence of the claims be shown. The Statute of Frauds is only a screening device; a party that has written proof of an agreement does not automatically prevail. Rather, the party must then proceed to prove its case on the merits (i.e., was there a breach? consideration? duress?). Thus, to say that a contract "falls within" the Statute simply means that it will only be enforced if it is in writing and the plaintiff prevails on the merits. Conversely, a contract that "falls outside" the Statute is one that can be enforced without written documentation if the plaintiff wins on the merits. Moreover, oral contracts that fall within the Statute are enforced on grounds of equity (fairness) in some circumstances.

I. CONTRACTS WITHIN THE STATUTE OF FRAUDS:

The following types of contracts fall within the Statute of Frauds:

Mnemonic: **MAD GLO**

A. Marriage was consideration for promise.
B. Administrator or Executor.
C. Debt of another (suretyship).

D. Goods which sell for more than $500. (under common law, or UCC applies to contracts between merchants)
E. Land
F. One year provision.

These provisions are not mutually exclusive and are detailed below.

A. Contracts Made in Consideration of Marriage (Rest. 2d. § 124)
A promise to give or pay property in exchange for marriage is unenforceable unless written. If no property is involved (e.g., A promises to marry B "in exchange for" B promising to marry A), there is no writing requirement.

B. Administrator or Executor (Rest. 2d. § 111)
A promise by an administrator or executor of an estate to *personally* pay the debts of the estate must be in writing to be enforceable.

C. Debt of Another/Suretyship (Rest. 2d. § 110)
A promise to pay the debts or defaults of another (suretyship agreement) is enforceable only if written. To fall within the Statute a suretyship must have the following elements:

1. Secondary Liability
The promisor/guarantor must be only secondarily liable for another's debt. Example: B tells C to deliver a boat to A. If B intends to pay for the boat in the case that A defaults, then the agreement is a surety and has to be in writing. But if B tells C to charge the purchase price to his account, then there is no suretyship, and an oral promise is enforceable.

2. Promisee's Awareness
The promisee-creditor must be aware or have reason to know that a suretyship relationship existed between the parties, and the promise must be made to the creditor directly. If the creditor does not know that a suretyship existed, the promises are enforceable, even if they are oral. The reason for this rule is to protect a creditor from being tricked into relying on a party's oral promise, which is actually a surety that requires writing to be enforceable.

3. Novation
A novation is a promise to pay the debt of a third party which is given in exchange for a promise that the third party will no longer be liable. Novations are outside the Statute of Frauds and valid if oral.

4. Main-Purpose Rule (Rest. 2d. § 116)
In order for a promise of suretyship to fall within the Statute of Frauds, the main purpose of the promisor must have been to benefit the third party whose debts he guarantees. If a promisor acts to further his own interests, such a promise is enforceable even if oral. Usually, the issue of who benefits from the promisor's guarantee can be determined by looking at the consideration that is given in return for it.

D. Sale of Goods for More than $500 (UCC § 2-201(a))
Any contract for the sale of goods (including securities) which are for $500 or more, must be in writing. Exceptions: There are sale of goods contracts for $500 or more that are enforceable if unwritten:

Mnemonic: **SAG**

1. Specifically Manufactured Goods not Suitable for Others
An oral agreement/promise involving unique goods which are specially manufactured is enforceable. (UCC § 2-201(3)(a).) Rationale: A seller would not produce these goods if there was no agreement, because there is no market for them.

2. Admission by Party Against Whom Enforcement is Sought
If a party admits that an agreement existed, no written memorandum is required. However, the contract is limited to those terms (i.e., quantity) that are admitted. (UCC § 2-201(3).)

3. Goods Accepted or Paid for by the Buyer
No written evidence is needed with respect to goods that have been paid for or have been received and accepted. (UCC § 2-201(3)(c).)

E. Interest in Land (Rest. 2d. § 125)
A contract for the sale or purchase of an interest in land must be in writing to be enforceable.

1. Types of interests:

   Mnemonic: **MELT**

   a. <u>M</u>ortgages
      A promise to give a mortgage as security for a loan must be in writing. However, assigning rights of a mortgage is valid if orally done.

   b. <u>E</u>asements

   c. <u>L</u>eases
      Some states allow oral leases of less than one year duration.

   d. <u>T</u>imber
      Contracts for sale of timber must be written if buyer will cut wood after title to the land passes to him. Contracts involving minerals, oil, etc., must be in writing if minerals are to be removed.

2. A contract that incidentally involves land (e.g., to build a house or to lend money to buy land) does not fall under this provision.

3. Part Performance
   An initially unenforceable oral land contract may become binding if the parties act in reliance upon it.

   a. A vendor who conveys land under an oral contract can recover the contract price.

   b. A vendee who acts in reliance upon an oral land contract (e.g., improves the land, takes possession, or pays taxes on the land) can have the contract enforced.

F. Performance Takes Longer than <u>O</u>ne Year (Rest. 2d. § 130)
A contract that, by its terms, cannot be performed within one year is unenforceable if it is not written.

1. The one-year period begins to run from the date the contract is formed, not the date set for beginning performance.

2. One-Year Duration
   For a contract to fall under this provision of the Statute of Frauds, performance in less than a year must be impossible. This requires more than an expectation that it is highly unlikely that a contract will actually be performed within a year. The basic issue is whether, theoretically, the agreed performance could occur within a year, even if the contract expressly provides a longer duration.

   a. Performance v. Discharge
      The fact that a contract could be discharged within a year (by impossibility of performance, death of one of the parties, etc.) does not mean that the contract is taken out of the one-year provision.

      i. If the contract is prematurely terminated by some event and its principal purpose has been fulfilled, the performance requirement is met. Example: A promises to hire B for the duration of B's life. B could die within a year, so the contract is outside the Statute of Frauds because the main purpose, to hire B for life, has been achieved.

      ii. A premature death will satisfy the performance requirement if the death of a party will not mean that full performance was not rendered. Example: A promises to support B, a minor, until B is 18 years old. If B died within a year, A would still be considered to have met his obligation, so the contract is outside the Statute. However, if A hires B to sing in a club for five years, and B dies within a year, his obligation was not met and the contract still falls within the Statute.

b. Termination

i. A contract that may not be completed within a year but could be terminated within that time is covered by the Statute and must be written.

ii. The courts are split as to whether contracts that cannot be performed in one year, but allow either party the right to terminate (so that it could theoretically end within a year), are covered by the Statute of Frauds.

II. ELEMENTS REQUIRED TO SATISFY THE STATUTE OF FRAUDS

A. A written contract or memorandum must contain the following elements to satisfy the Statute of Frauds (Rest. 2d. § 131):

1. Purpose of the contract.

2. Terms and conditions of the agreement (essential terms).

3. Parties to the contract.

4. Consideration.

5. Signature of the party to be charged. A party's initials or stamped or typed name may also suffice.

A written memorandum that contains the above elements will satisfy the Statute even if it was not created for that purpose.

B. UCC § 2-201 Requirements

1. Under the UCC, which applies to sale-of-goods contracts, the requirements of a written memorandum are satisfied if a writing is;

a. Sufficient to indicate that a contract for sale has been made between the parties, *and*

b. Signed by the party against whom enforcement is sought.

2. A writing that omits or erroneously states a term is still valid, but the agreement is only enforceable as to the quantity of goods stated in the memorandum.

3. A memorandum that omits a price term may be enforceable if the parties can introduce collateral evidence as to the agreed upon price or if the court will imply such a term. (UCC § 2-305.)

4. An unsigned, written *confirmation* of an oral agreement that is sent *between merchants* will satisfy the Statute if it is received, the party receiving it knows or should know of its contents, and the party does not object to it within ten days. (UCC § 2-201(2).)

III. CONTRACTS THAT VIOLATE THE STATUTE OF FRAUDS

A contract that does not satisfy the requirements of the Statute will be either voidable, at the option of the parties, or void, depending on the jurisdiction.

A. If only part of the contract is within the Statute, the entire contract is unenforceable if that part does not satisfy the Statute. This rule does not hold, however, if the portion within the Statute has already been fully performed.

B. Full Performance

As a general rule, any oral contract that has been fully performed will be enforced. Example: A orally promises to work for B for 2 years and has completed performance. The contract is enforceable. Contracts for the sale of goods are enforceable for the amount of goods that have been accepted or paid for.

C. Alternative Promises

A party that promises to perform any of several alternative performances, some of which violate the Statute of Frauds, can be bound to perform those that do not.

IV. MODIFICATION AND RESCISSION

A written agreement can be orally rescinded. However, modification of an existing contract will be effective only if it satisfies the requirements of the contract (i.e., if this is a type of contract that has to be written, then the modification must also be written). An invalid oral modification of a contract leaves the original contract in effect without the changes. However, material reliance on an oral modification may make it enforceable to avoid injustice. (Rest. 2d. § 150.)

V. REMEDIES

A party that has partly performed under a contract that is later invalidated by the Statute of Frauds is entitled to certain remedies.

A. Unjust Enrichment

A party that confers benefits upon another is entitled to restitution for those benefits if the contract is later voided. A plaintiff can recover the market value (as opposed to contract price) of his performance if he can prove it. If the defendant is willing to perform, then there are no restitution damages. Additionally, a party can sometimes recover the value of acts done in reliance upon the contract. Example: A moves to New York to fulfill his oral agreement with B. A may be able to recover his moving expenses.

B. Promissory Estoppel

A court will sometimes enforce an "invalid" oral contract on its terms if it was foreseeable that the defendant's conduct would cause the plaintiff to change his position in reliance on the oral contract. Usually, if a defendant has willfully lied by saying that the contract was not subject to the Statute of Frauds, or that he would not raise the Statute as an objection, a court will enforce the oral contract. In some cases, if a plaintiff performs his obligations without any fraudulent inducement, a court may enforce the promise so as to avoid injustice. (Rest. 2d. § 139.)

CASE CLIPS

Harry Rubin & Sons v. Consolidated Pipe Co. (1959)

Facts: Rubin claimed he made three oral contracts, each in excess of $500, to order plastic hoops from the defendant, a manufacturer. Rubin introduced three writings in court. The first was the order form for the first shipment, the second was a letter that stated, in part, "that upon completion of the [first] order," Consolidated will produce the second order. Finally, Rubin sent a confirmation of the last order, which included the size, quantity, and price of the items desired.
Issue: Does a written memorandum confirming an oral agreement satisfy the requirements of the Statute of Frauds?
Rule: A writing that affords a basis for believing that the offered oral evidence rests on a real transaction satisfies the Statute of Frauds. Under UCC § 2-201(2) an unsigned written confirmation of an oral agreement is satisfactory if it is between merchants and (1) it is sent within a reasonable time after the oral agreement was made; (2) it is sufficient to bind the sender; (3) it is received; (4) there is no reply though the recipient has reason to know of its contents; and (5) no objection is made within ten days of its receipt, although the recipient had reason to know of its contents.

Monarco v. Lo Greco (1950)

Facts: Lo Greco was orally promised by his mother and stepfather that he would inherit their farm if he remained on the site and managed its operations. He did so and helped raised the value of the farm from about $4,000 to $100,000 over 20 years. However, his stepfather decided to will the farm to a grandson, Monarco. The California Statute of Frauds provided that agreements not to be performed during the life of the promisor are not valid unless written.

Issue: Under the doctrine of promissory estoppel, may a party be estopped from relying upon the defense of the Statute of Frauds?
Rule: A promise, which the promisor should reasonably expect to induce action or forbearance on the part of the promisee or a third person, and which does induce the action or forbearance, is enforceable, notwithstanding the Statute of Frauds, if injustice can only be avoided by enforcing the promise.

Warder & Lee Elevator, Inc. v. Britten (1979)

Facts: Lee, a grain broker, entered into an oral contract to buy crops for an amount in excess of $500, from Britten, a farmer. The parties had previously made several such oral agreements which were fully performed. In reliance upon having future delivery of Britten's grain, Lee contracted to sell to a third party. Britten reneged, claiming the contract was unenforceable because it violated the Statute of Frauds.
Issue: In a UCC context, can a contract that violates the Statue of Frauds be enforced on grounds of promissory estoppel?
Rule: Even when an oral contract fails the UCC Statute of Frauds provision, the doctrine of promissory estoppel may still be applied through § 1-103 which provides that the "principles of law and equity . . . shall supplement these provisions."

Lige Dickson Co. v. Union Oil Co. of Cal (1981) Note Case

Facts: Lige Dickson used liquid asphalt supplied by Union Oil in its business as a paving contractor. In 1971, Union Oil promised Lige Dickson that any future price increases would not apply to jobs Lige Dickson had already contracted to do. Union Oil later attempted to raise its prices in violation of its "guarantee."
Issue: Can a contract that violates the UCC Statute of Frauds be enforced on grounds of promissory estoppel?
Rule: Promissory estoppel cannot be used to overcome the statute of frauds in a case involving the sale of goods.
Note: This case conflicts with *Warder & Lee* and demonstrates the conflicting views of the courts on this issue.

C.R. Fedrick, Inc. v. Borg-Warner Corp. (1977)

Facts: Borg made an oral offer by phone to sell pumps to Fedrick, a contractor. Fedrick used the bid to calculate its own bid on a large project that it was subsequently awarded. Borg then refused to sell at

its quoted price, claiming the agreement violated the Statute of Frauds.
Issue: Can the Statute of Frauds be circumvented by assertion of promissory estoppel?
Rule: Although promissory estoppel can be used as an exception to the Statute of Frauds, this rule does not extend to a vendor's oral bid for the sale and delivery of goods, which must be reduced to a writing as required by the Statute of Frauds.

Chapter 4

POLICING THE BARGAIN

I. CAPACITY TO CONTRACT

Certain classes of individuals lack full capacity to contract. Contracts they form are often voidable at their option.

A. Minors

Minors can disaffirm any contract, except for necessities, during minority and within a reasonable time after reaching majority. (Rest. 2d. § 14.)

1. Exceptions are statutory or involve contracts that deal with duties imposed by law (e.g., marriage contract, agreement to support an illegitimate child).

2. Upon a minor's disaffirmance, the non-infant party is limited to restitution, and only if the minor still possesses the goods.

3. A minor can ratify after a contract coming of age, expressly or by conduct that causes reliance by the other party.

B. Mental Incompetents

Mentally incompetent parties can disaffirm a contract if, by reason of mental illness or defect,

1. They are unable to understand in a reasonable manner the nature and consequences of the transaction, or

2. They are unable to act in a reasonable manner in relation to the transaction, and

3. The other party has reason to know of the condition. (Rest. 2d. § 15.)

C. An intoxicated party can also avoid contractual duties if he does not understand the transaction (majority rule).

II. INEQUALITY OF EXCHANGE

A. An unequal exchange will not usually void a contract in an action *at law*, especially if the parties deal at arm's length.

B. Courts will deny equitable relief (i.e., specific performance) to protect a party that refuses to perform its part of a highly disproportionate exchange.

C. The adequacy of consideration is judged as of the time of the transaction. Example: In an arm's-length agreement, A promises to sell ten law guides to B in exchange for $100. The goods are to be delivered and paid for in 30 days. To the surprise of both parties, the fair market value of law guides increases to $1,000 each by the date of the actual exchange. Although the consideration is vastly disproportionate at the time of the actual exchange, it was adequate at the time the contract was made.

III. REVISIONS OF CONTRACTUAL DUTY

A. Pre-existing Duty Rule
If one party promises another that he will do what he is already legally obligated to do, the promise is not a detriment sufficient to satisfy the requirement of consideration. (Rest. 2d. § 73.)

1. Courts have held that modifications of rents and wages are invalid because of a pre-existing duty.

2. Foakes v. Beer Rule
An agreement to accept payment of a lesser sum on or after the due date of a money debt is not binding for lack of consideration.

    a. This rule is severely criticized because it discourages settlements. It has been overruled in some jurisdictions.

b. Most jurisdictions follow it, but hold that sufficient detriment exists if payment of a lesser sum is accompanied by some additional act of the debtor.

3. Pre-existing Duty Rule Not Applicable:

a. Original contract is rescinded and a new contract is executed, with the mutual promises serving again as consideration.

b. Contract modification is a partial rescission and therefore supported by consideration (Watkins & Sons v. Carrig).

c. Some new detriment can be found for consideration.

d. Rest. 2d. § 89(a) allows a modification to be binding if compelled by unforseen circumstances.

e. Under promissory estoppel, a modification is binding to the extent that justice requires enforcement because of reliance on the modification.

f. Some state statutes allow modifications without consideration as long as written and signed.

g. UCC § 2-209(1) repudiated the rule by providing that a modification requires no consideration to be binding.

h. Dropping an invalid claim serves in most courts as consideration for modification if the party has a genuine and reasonable subjective belief that the surrendered claim is valid.

4. Third-party Situations
If C, an outsider to the contract, promises compensation to a party to fulfill a contract with another,

a. Majority holds that the agreement with C is invalid since the party is merely promising to perform his legal obligation.

b. Minority, which includes the Restatement, holds that a valid contract with C is formed.

B. Economic Duress

1. Rule
A contract is voidable if a party was forced to agree to it by use of a wrongful threat precluding his exercise of free will.

2. Proof
A party must show that immediate possession of needful goods is threatened and that the goods could not be obtained from another source.

3. Remedy is usually restitution.

4. Exercise of a legal right, such as the right to dispute the value of services, is not economic duress.

C. Check Tendered as Payment in Full

1. Common-law Rule
If there is a good-faith dispute over the amount of a debt and the debtor tenders a check for a lesser amount than creditor's claim, cashing the check, even "under protest," discharges the debt.

a. A debtor's intention that the check be full satisfaction of the debt must be clearly indicated to the creditor.

b. Partial payment by a fiduciary (an agent who holds the assets of another) will not result in an accord and satisfaction.

2. UCC § 1-207

   a. A creditor can cash a check tendered as "payment in full" and still reserve the right to sue for the balance of the debt by writing words of protest on the check.

   b. This rule protects creditors.

   c. Some jurisdictions ignore this rule because it makes settlement of claims difficult.

IV. OVERREACHING IN THE BARGAINING PROCESS

A. Concealment

1. In the absence of a fiduciary relationship, there is no liability for bare nondisclosure of known latent defects.

2. However, half-truths are actionable as whole lies and grounds for contract rescission.

B. Misrepresentation

1. Innocent misrepresentations (i.e., negligent, unintentional) are actionable.

2. The misrepresentation must be of a material factor in the contract.

3. The complainant must show justifiable reliance.

4. The misrepresentation must be of facts, not opinions or law.

   a. Opinion is actionable if a fiduciary relationship exists.

   b. Restrictions on relief from misrepresentations of law and opinion are increasingly being relaxed. There is a disposition to treat the nature of the statement (fact or opinion) as only one part of the broader issue of whether reliance was justified.

C. Confidential Relation
A confidential relation is grounds for avoiding a contract if it is used to contravene the bargaining process.

1. Exemplary relationships include guardian and ward, principal and agent, doctor and patient, etc.

2. A confidential relation is deemed to exist whenever the relative positions of the parties gives one the power and means to take advantage or exert undue influence over the other.

3. Factors that determine such a relation are disparities in age, education, or business experience.

4. If the claimant in an action is the party in whom confidence was placed, he must prove that the bargain was fair and at arm's length (without a confidential relation, however, fraud is not presumed).

D. Relief from Mistake (Rest. 2d. § 152)

1. Mutual Mistake

a. The mistake under which both parties are acting must have a material effect on the agreed exchange.

i. Proof that one would not have entered the contract but for the mistake is not sufficient.

ii. It must be unfair to require performance.

iii. Availability of other remedies may lead a court to decide that the mistake's effect is not "material."

b. The mistake must involve a basic assumption.

   i. Determinative factors are the magnitude of the mistake, the degree of certainty in the minds of the parties, and the attitude toward the type of transaction involved.

   ii. Belief that the thing bargained for in the contract actually exists is considered to be a basic assumption.

   iii. Courts are divided as to whether the quality of the agreement's subject matter is a basic assumption (*Sherwood v. Walker, Wood v. Boynton*).

c. The adversely affected party must not "bear the risk of the mistake." (Rest. 2d §§ 152, 154.)

   i. Risk can be allocated by the contract terms.

   ii. Risk is allocated to a party if he enters a contract despite having doubts about the facts to which the mistake relates.

   iii. Risk can be allocated by the court if it is reasonable to do so.

   iv. Negligent failure of a party to know or discover facts as to which both parties are under a mistake does not preclude rescission (*Beachcomber Coins, Inc. v. Boskett*).

d. Remedy: Usually, rescission of the contract.

2. Unilateral Mistake (Rest. 2d, § 153)

   a. Courts are less willing to grant rescission in cases where only one party is mistaken because the remedy deprives the non-mistaken party of the benefit of the bargain.

b. Elements:

   i. Unilateral mistake requires the same three elements that are needed for mutual mistake: basic assumption, material effect on the exchange, and the risk must not have been allocated to the adversely affected party, **and**

   ii. Either the enforcement of the agreement would be unconscionable, or the other party had reason to know of the mistake or actually caused it.

c. Courts are more likely to grant rescission for a clerical error than a mistake in judgment (*Elsinore Union Elementary Sch. Dist. v. Kastorff*).

3. Warranty

   a. Parties that try to avoid a contract by pleading concealment or mistake sometimes have the option of claiming breach of warranty (implied or express).

   b. Warranty analysis is used mostly in sale-of-goods cases.

      a. Look to UCC § 2-312.

      b. The risk of mistake is placed on the seller unless the warranty is excluded in the contract pursuant to the code's provisions.

      c. Implied warranties were recently extended to personal injury claims and to transactions involving the sale of houses.

V. UNCONSCIONABILITY AND ADHESION CONTRACTS

A. Unconscionability

The doctrine of unconscionability is used to avoid oppression and unfair surprise, but not to disturb the allocation of risk in contract formation. (UCC § 2-302, comment 1.)

1. UCC § 2-302:

   a. Judges decide the issue of unconscionability as a matter of law.

   b. Unconscionability is determined by circumstances at the time the contract was made.

   c. Parties are entitled to a reasonable opportunity to present evidence of the circumstances ("commercial setting, purpose and effect") to aid the court in making its decision.

   d. The doctrine is used mostly in consumer cases, but there are occasional business applications (e.g., *Gianni Sport Ltd. v. Gantos, Inc.*).

   e. Rest. 2d. § 208, using similar language as UCC § 2-302, allows a court to refuse to enforce all or part of an unconscionable agreement.

2. Types of Unconscionability

   a. Procedural
   Unfairness in the bargaining process. Courts usually require some kind of procedural unconscionability before refusing to enforce a contract.

   b. Substantive
   Unfairness in the bargaining outcome. Substantive unconscionability is criticized for interfering with the private right to contract at arm's length.

i. Unconscionability has been recognized to include an absence of meaningful choice on the part of one of the parties, together with contract terms that are unreasonably favorable to the other party. (See *Williams v. Walker-Thomas Furniture Co.*)

ii. Courts have used price unconscionability, a type of substantive unconscionability, to invalidate agreements. (See *Jones v. Star Credit Corp.*)

c. Waiver of defenses and cross-collateral clauses has been found unconscionable.

3. Remedies
If the agreement, or part of it, is unconscionable, the court may

a. Refuse to enforce the whole contract,

b. Refuse to enforce the unconscionable part of the contract, or

c. Limit the application of any unconscionable clause to avoid any unconscionable result.

d. When Remedies are Limited:

i. UCC § 2-719(2)
When a limited remedy "fails of its essential purpose" because of the circumstances, "remedy may be had as provided in this Act." The Comment states that this section is to be applied when the limitation of the remedy works in an "unconscionable manner." (See *Wilson Trading, Corp. v. David Ferguson, Ltd.*)

ii. UCC § 2-719(3)
Consequential damages may be limited or excluded, unless the limitation or exclusion is unconscionable. Limitation of consequential damages for personal

injury in a consumer-goods case is *prima facie* unconscionable.

B. Standard Form Contracts (Contracts of Adhesion)

1. Primary Advantages:

   a. Save time and reduce uncertainty

   b. Allow parties to control risks

2. Courts will void provisions in form contracts which were not actually understood and agreed to by the party not writing (*Henningsen v. Bloomfield Motors*).

3. Unconscionability will invalidate a form-contract provision if a stronger party uses his superior bargaining power to introduce contract provisions that cause the lesser party great hardship.

4. Nondrafters usually do not realize that printed slips and tickets are contracts to limit the liability of the issuer.

   a. Rest. 2d. § 212 deals with this difficulty, providing that a paper binds a party only if he "signs or otherwise manifests assent."

   b. If the issuer has reason to believe that the party manifesting assent would not do so if he knew that the writing contained a particular term, the term is not part of the agreement. (Rest. 2d. § 211(3).)

5. Measures for Reducing the Problems of Adhesion

   a. Legislation, which is usually aimed at correcting imbalances of bargaining power.

i. Statutes require contracts to be written in "plain language" and regulations to control the terms of the exchange and remedies.

ii. The main problem with such statutes is inflexibility.

b. Judicial Control
Judicial control is more flexible, but incapable of revising underlying patterns of market relationships.

c. Administrative Control
Administrative control creates quasi-judicial responsibility and power within a limited jurisdiction (i.e., investigate charges against common carriers and control over contract terms in insurance contracts). Administrative control is fairly flexible because administrative decisions are of lesser precedential value than judicial decisions.

C. Home-solicitation Sales

1. State statutes provide a cooling-off period, during which a buyer can cancel his purchase.

2. Uniform Consumer Credit Code allows the buyer to cancel "until midnight of the third business day" after a home-solicitation sale.

VI. ILLEGALITY

A. Courts will also void agreements that are valid from the perspective of contract law, but are otherwise in violation of public policy (illegal contracts).

B. Criminal sanctions are a more effective way to handle illegal agreements.

C. Claims for restitution are usually precluded, but sometimes allowed if,

1. The claimant is not *in pari delicto* (equally blameworthy) with the defendant, or

2. The claimant is *in locus poenitentiae* (withdrew before consummation of the illegal bargain).

D. Remitter's Liability
A mere agent or depository of the proceeds of an illegal transaction is not permitted to assert the defense of illegality in an action to recover the proceeds by a party to the illegal transaction.

E. Types of Illegal Contracts and Effects of Illegality:

1. Covenants Not to Compete
Unless made in bad faith, courts enforce such covenants up to the point that is reasonably necessary to protect the employer's interest without imposing undue hardship on the employee.

2. Inducing Official Action

   a. Contingent fee arrangements for services in securing the passage of legislation are strictly scrutinized.

   b. Contingent fees for lawyers are permissible because they ensure the most humble citizen equal justice under the law.

3. Bribery

   a. A contract in which an employee is bribed to take official action is illegal and unenforceable. Most courts will not enforce such a contract even if one party was unjustly enriched.

   b. Sometimes if a party bribes a third party in order to help him perform his obligations under a contract, the contract will not be enforced if public policy is strongly frustrated.

4. Licensing
   If the purpose of a licensing requirement is protection of the public, the want of a license will render the contract for the unlicensed services unenforceable (e.g., uncertified doctor, lawyer, etc.).

5. Usury
   Loan agreements that charge interest rates in excess of the legal limit are unenforceable.

6. Wagering
   Although courts are unwilling to enforce private gambling contracts, they will grant restitution if

   a. The claimant is not *in pari delicto* with the defendant, or

   b. The claimant was *in locus poenitentiae*.

CASE CLIPS

Kiefer v. Fred Howe Motors, Inc. (1968)

Facts: Kiefer, a married man with a young child, bought a car when he was just under 21 years old. He later became dissatisfied with the car and sought to rescind the contract.
Issue: May one rescind a contract on the grounds that it was made while he was still a minor?
Rule: A contract made by a minor, other than for necessities, is either void or voidable at his option because minors require some protection from the pitfalls of the marketplace.

Ortelere v. Teachers' Retirement Bd. (1969)

Facts: Ortelere's wife, a teacher, built up a reserve of $70,925 in the public retirement system. Ortelere quit his job to care for his wife when she suffered a nervous breakdown. Two months before she died, while suffering from mental illness, Ortelere's wife exercised an irrevocable option to take maximum retirement benefits, depriving him of any right to the remaining portion of her retirement fund at her death.

Issue: Is a contract voidable if a contracting party cannot act reasonably due to mental incapacity?

Rule: A party incurs only voidable contractual duties by entering into a transaction if, by reason of mental illness or defect, it is unable to act in a reasonable manner in relation to the transaction and the other party has reason to know of its condition.

Cundick v. Broadbent (1967)

Facts: Cundick sold ranch lands and other property to Broadbent, for less than half its market value. The contract was later amended to pay an additional sum which was still less than full value. When the sale had almost been completed, Cundick's wife sued to rescind the contract. Three years prior to entering into the contract, Cundick had received psychiatric treatment but nothing further had been said or done about any mental condition until the suit was commenced.

Issue: Is mere weakness of mind sufficient mental incompetency to render a contract voidable?

Rule: Mental capacity to contract depends upon whether the allegedly disabled person possessed sufficient reason to enable him to understand the nature and effect of the act in issue. Average intelligence is not essential to a valid bargain.

McKinnon v. Benedict (1968)

Facts: McKinnon loaned Benedict $5,000, interest free, to buy a resort adjoining McKinnon's property in return for Benedict's promise not to make new improvements on the land between the resort and his property for 25 years. After Benedict repaid the loan, he decided to build a trailer park and tent camp because he was losing money on the property. McKinnon sued in equity to enjoin this activity. The camping facilities were not visible from McKinnon's house during the summer months when McKinnon actually lived there.

Issue: Is a contract that exchanges substantial restrictions for relatively minimal consideration enforceable in equity?

Rule: Inadequacy of consideration, minimal benefit to the party imposing the restrictions, and the oppressive nature of restrictions can combine to make a contract unreasonable and unenforceable in equity.

Tuckwiller v. Tuckwiller (1967)

Facts: Tuckwiller agreed to care for an ailing, 73-year-old woman who had promised to bequeath her house and farm to her. The woman died soon afterward without changing her will and before Tuckwiller had provided her with much care. She did, however, have the ambulance attendants witness a paper that contained her promise. Tuckwiller sued the executor of the estate for specific performance of the promise.

Issue: Should the court measure the adequacy of consideration at the time the contract was made or at the time of the alleged breach?

Rule: In determining whether a contract is so unfair, inequitable, or unconscionable as to warrant denial of specific performance, the transaction must be viewed prospectively, not retrospectively. Viewed in this light, prior services and the past relations of the parties may properly be considered in connection with the fairness of the contract and adequacy of the consideration. In the instant case the fact that the woman tried to change her will revealed her satisfaction with the bargain.

Black Indus. Inc. v. Bush (1953)

Facts: Bush contracted to produce and sell mechanical parts to Black Industries, who resold them at a large profit. The assembled parts were ultimately sold to the government. Bush refused to perform, claiming that Black Industries was receiving excessive profits in violation of public policy since the government was the ultimate purchaser.

Issue: Is a contract void as being against public policy if there is no evidence of fraud?

Rule: A contract that is made freely and without evidence of fraud, is not void as against public policy unless it violates recognized legal principles. The validity of the contract is not affected by the relative values of the consideration in a contract between businessmen dealing at arm's length.

Schwartzreich v. Bauman-Basch, Inc. (1921)

Facts: Schwartzreich contracted to work for Bauman-Bausch for one year at $90 a week. Before beginning work, Schwartzreich was offered $115 a week by another employer. Bauman-Basch offered to raise his weekly salary to $100, and Schwartzreich accepted. Another contract was made, reflecting the new salary provision, and the old one was simultaneously torn up. Bauman-Basch fired him before the year passed, claiming the second contract was unenforceable due to lack of consideration.

Issue: Is a new contract that replaces a prior contract with terms that are similar, but more favorable to one party, enforceable?

Rule: When an existing contract is terminated by mutual consent and a new one is executed in its place, the mutual promises of the parties constitute consideration. Any changes to an existing contract must have new consideration to support it.

Arzani v. People (1956)

Facts: The state of New York contracted with Kranz and Martin for the reconstruction of a highway. Kranz and Martin entered into a written subcontract with Arzani to do part of the work. Succumbing to union pressure for a wage increase, the plaintiff told the general contractors that he could not complete the job unless they shared the increased labor cost. Kranz orally agreed to pay half. Following the completion of the project, Arzani sued the state and general contractors to recover this amount.

Issue: Is a promise made to induce the performance of a preexisting duty enforceable?

Rule: Absent new consideration, a promise made to induce the performance of a preexisting duty to perform is unenforceable.

Watkins & Son v. Carrig (1941)

Facts: Watkins & Son contracted to excavate a cellar for Carrig. After work began, Watkins & Son encountered solid rock and Carrig orally agreed to pay nine times the original excavation price. Carrig later reneged, claiming his promise was unenforceable due to lack of consideration (i.e., there was a pre-existing duty to do the work anyway).

Issue: Is a modification of an agreement unenforceable because of a lack of consideration?

Rule: Modification involves a partial rescission of the prior contract and therefore the promise to do the original work is new consideration.

Note: After classifying modification as a "partial rescission" of the original contract, the court used same analysis as seen above in *Schwartzreich v. Bauman-Basch, Inc.*

Austin Instrument, Inc. v. Loral Corp. (1971)

Facts: Loral had a contract to produce radar sets for the Navy. The sets had 40 component parts, of which Austin, a subcontractor, produced 23. When Loral received a second contract from the Navy, Austin bid on all 40 parts. Loral informed Austin that it would only receive the subcontract for the parts on which it was the low bidder. Austin threatened to stop delivery of the parts on the first contract if it did not receive a price increase and the subcontract for all 40 parts of the second contract. After unsuccessfully checking with all the other subcontractors on its approved list, Loral agreed to Austin's demands so as to avoid breaching its contract with the Navy.

Issue: Is a contract modification enforceable if it was agreed to by a party who was deprived of free will under circumstances amounting to economic duress?

Rule: A contract is voidable if the party claiming duress was forced to agree by means of a wrongful threat precluding the exercise of his free will. The existence of economic duress is demonstrated by proof that immediate possession of needed goods is threatened and that the goods could not be obtained from another source.

Kibler v. Frank L. Garrett & Sons, Inc. (1968)

Facts: In response to a dispute over how much money he owed Kibler for harvesting wheat, Garret sent a check for what he felt he owed. A clause, written in fine print, stated that cashing the check would constitute full satisfaction of the debt. Kibler accepted the check without noticing the fine print and sued for the rest of the debt.

Issue: When there is a dispute over the amount of a debt, must the party alleging full satisfaction demonstrate that he actually manifested his intention to the other party that he would pay no more than the amount submitted?

Rule: When partial payment of a debated debt is intended to be full satisfaction, it must be clearly brought to the attention of the payee.

Marton Remodeling v. Jensen (1985)

Facts: Jensen hired Marton to do remodeling work on his home. The parties disagreed over the amount of the bill. Jensen sent a check for a smaller sum with the condition that endorsement of the check on the back by Marton would constitute full satisfaction. Marton cashed the check after writing "not full payment" on it and sued for the balance owed.

Issue: Has an accord and satisfaction occurred if a check marked "payment in full" is cashed with express protest?

Rule: An accord and satisfaction occurs even if a "payment in full" check is cashed under protest.

Note: According to this court, UCC § 1-207 does not displace the common law rule of accord and satisfaction. This is, however, a contested area of the law.

Swinton v. Whitinsville Sav. Bank (1942)

Facts: The Whitinsville Bank knew the house that Swinton was purchasing from it was infected by termites but it did not disclose this information to Swinton.

Issue: Is a party to a contract obligated to reveal known latent defects to the other party?

Rule: There is no liability for bare nondisclosure when parties deal at arm's length, provided a false representation or attempt to conceal the condition was not made.

Kannavos v. Annino (1969)

Facts: Annino converted her single family home into a multi-family apartment building and then sold it to Kannavos without telling him its use violated city zoning laws. Kannavos sued to rescind the contract after the city moved to abate the use of the building.

Issue: Can a sales contract be rescinded when a seller knowingly concealed material facts, if the buyer could have discovered the truth by examining public records?

Rule: If a seller speaks with reference to a given subject, voluntarily or at the buyer's request, and knowingly conceals material facts bearing on that subject, the buyer can rescind the contract, even though he did not check the public records where the truth could have been ascertained.

Beachcomber Coins, Inc. v. Boskett (1979)

Facts: Beachcomber, a coin dealer, sought rescission of a coin purchase from Boskett. At the time of purchase neither party knew that the coin was actually counterfeit. Beachcomber had inspected the coin prior to buying.
Issue: Is a contract voidable for a mutual mistake of fact?
Rule: A contract is voidable by either party when both parties are under a misapprehension regarding a fact assumed by both as the basis of their transaction. Moreover, negligent failure of a party to know or discover the erroneous fact does not preclude rescission.

O'Callaghan v. Waller and Beckwith Realty Co. (1958)

Facts: O'Callaghan was injured, due to her landlord's negligence in maintaining and operating the apartment building. A clause in the lease exculpated the landlord from liability for his own negligence.
Issue: Is a contract with an exculpatory clause which relieves a party from the consequences of its own negligence void as against public policy?
Rule: Contracts with exculpatory clauses are generally enforced unless it is against settled public policy or there is something in the social relationship of the parties that militates against upholding the agreement.
Note: The court held that this exculpatory clause was enforceable but current law generally does not allow such clauses in landlord-tenant agreements.

Henningsen v. Bloomfield Motors, Inc. (1960)

Facts: Henningsen purchased a new car from Bloomfield Motors. His wife was injured when the steering failed ten days after the car was delivered. All implied warranties of merchantability were disclaimed by a clause buried in the fine print on the back of the contract.
Issue: In an adhesion contract, can a manufacturer or dealer disclaim all warranties of merchantability?
Rule: When there is vastly unequal bargaining power between the parties to a contract, contract clauses that disclaim the implied warranty of merchantability are void as against public policy.
Note: An adhesion contract is one in which a party is forced to accept the terms of the other because of unequal bargaining power.

Wilson Trading Corporation v. David Ferguson, Ltd. (1968)

Facts: David Ferguson bought yarn from Wilson Trading and used it to make sweaters. After washing the sweaters, it was discovered that the color was uneven, making them "unmerchantable." The contract provided that the yarn would be merchantable. However, the contract also disclaimed liability for defects discovered after "weaving, knitting, or processing" of the yarn. Wilson Trading sued when David Ferguson refused to pay.

Issue: Can a contract bar all claims for defects after a certain specified time limitation period has expired?

Rule: Although parties to a contract are given latitude to fashion their own remedies for breach, these provisions are subject to UCC § 2-719(2), which substitutes remedies provided by the UCC for agreed to terms that are inadequate. Under UCC § 2-607(3) a buyer is given reasonable time after he discovers or should have discovered a defect, to assert a claim. Furthermore, the contract provision that creates an unlimited express warranty of merchantability, which includes latent defects, must prevail over the time limitation provision insofar as the latter modifies the former. (UCC § 2-316(1).)

Note: The court suggested that a time limitation clause may be unconscionable, although it does not rely on UCC § 2-302.

Williams v. Walker-Thomas Furniture Co. (1965)

Facts: Walker-Thomas sold a number of household items to Williams, on an installment plan. The sales contract had an "add on" clause, which stated that all of Williams' purchases were consolidated into a single debt, and that any payment would be credited equally, among all the items. The effect of the clause is that Williams would only own an item after she has paid for *all* of them. In case of default the furniture was to be repossessed. Walker-Thomas sued to replevy the items, and Williams contested the contract.

Issue: Can a court refuse to enforce an unconscionable contract?

Rule: Where the element of unconscionability is present at the time the contract is made, the contract should not be enforced. Unconscionability has generally been recognized to include an absence of meaningful choice on the part of one of the parties in conjunction with contract terms unreasonably favorable to the other party. (UCC § 2-302.)

Jones v. Star Credit Corp. (1969)

Facts: The Jones, welfare recipients, contracted to pay $1,234.80 for a freezer that ordinarily retailed for less than $300. UCC § 2-302 provided that a court may refuse to enforce a contract or excise an objectionable clause if it finds that the contract or clause was unconscionable at the time it was made.

Issue: Can a contract be void for unconscionability because a price term is excessive?

Rule: Under UCC § 2-302, a court may refuse to enforce the contract, enforce the remainder of the contract without the term, or limit the application of any excessive price term on the grounds of unconscionability.

Hillesland v. Federal Land Bank Assoc. (1987)

Facts: Hillesland, CEO of a banking institution, was fired because of practices that damaged the image of the institution and its regulator. Hillesland's employment agreement was not for a specified or fixed duration.

Issue: Is there an implied covenant that a discharge will be made in good faith and fair dealing in at-will employment contracts?

Rule: The majority of states do not recognize an implied covenant of good faith and fair dealing in at-will employment contracts.

Central Adjustment Bureau, Inc. v. Ingram (1984)

Facts: Ingram and the other defendants were all former employees of Central Adjustment Bureau, a large collection agency. While at Central, they had signed noncompetition agreements which stated that they would not do similar work in the United States for two years after resignation and would not contact any parties who had been Central's clients during the time the defendants had been employed there. The defendants opened a similar business in violation of the agreement.

Issue: Can a court modify an unnecessarily broad noncompetition agreement to make it reasonable?

Rule: Unless an employer acts in bad faith, noncompetition covenants are enforceable to the extent that they are reasonably necessary to protect the employer's interests without imposing undue hardship on the employee. This approach of allowing partial enforcement of such covenants involves less variation from the intent of the parties than total nonenforcement would.

Sirkin v. Fourteenth Street Store (1908)

Facts: Sirkin sold and delivered hosiery and wrappers to the Fourteenth Street Store. The store claimed that Sirkin had bribed its purchasing agent to obtain the order. Such bribes were misdemeanors, punishable by fines and imprisonment. Sirkin sued when the store refused to pay.

Issue: Is a contract made in violation of a criminal statute enforceable if the goods have been delivered under the contract?

Rule: Illegal contracts that violate criminal laws are unenforceable, even if the terms of the agreement were carried out and nonenforcement causes unjust enrichment.

McConnell v. Commonwealth Pictures Corp. (1960)

Facts: Commonwealth Pictures contracted to pay McConnell $10,000 and a percentage of the profits if he succeeded in getting the distribution rights to a film for Commonwealth. He succeeded and was paid $10,000. Commonwealth, however, refused to pay the percentage of profits, claiming that he used bribery to get the distribution rights.

Issue: Is a legal contract enforceable if performed in an illegal manner?

Rule: A party is denied recovery, even on a contract that is valid on its face, if it appears that gravely immoral and illegal conduct was used to accomplish its performance. There must be a direct connection between the illegal conduct and the obligation sued upon.

Goldberg v. Sanglier (1982)

Facts: Sanglier, seeking to open a car dealership, was required to use "his own money." Goldberg and others invested the money knowing Sanglier would lie as to its source. He later gave Goldberg falsely gloomy reports of the business to encourage him to sell at a loss. Goldberg sued for fraud, and Sanglier raised the defense of in pari delicto (in equal guilt).

Issue: If the parties are not equally culpable, is the defense of in pari delicto appropriate?

Rule: When the parties are not equally culpable, the defense of in pari delicto is not appropriate.

Note: Deciding on the issue of in pari delicto is largely a public policy decision. Here, the court sought to deter future behavior of this nature and to prevent unjust enrichment.

Chapter 5

REMEDIES FOR BREACH

Once a contract has been made, the parties are obligated to perform their duties under the contract. However one party may refuse to perform for some reason and will thus breach the contract. The nonbreaching party can sue to recover the damages it incurred. Relief is available at law and in equity in a variety of forms. (Note: A party can recover in restitution the value of benefits conferred where no valid contract exists between the parties).

I. REMEDIES AT LAW

At law, the nonbreaching party is awarded monetary damages to compensate for the loss incurred. Courts seek to protect three interests when awarding monetary damages:

- Expectation
- Reliance (addressed in Chapter 1)
- Restitution (addressed in Chapter 1)

II. MEASURING EXPECTATION

Courts have a strong preference for awarding damages measured by the value of the expectation that the promise/contract created. The object is to put the party in the same position he would be in if the contract was performed as expected. This includes both the value of expenses incurred and expected profits.

A. Computing the Value of Expectations (Rest. 2d. § 347)

Professor Farnsworth's formula for calculating expectation damages is

General damages = Loss in value + other loss - cost avoided - loss avoided

1. Loss in Value

    a. The difference between the *value to the injured party* of the performance he should have received and that of any performance he did receive. Example: If the defendant paid the plaintiff $100 of a $1,000 debt, the loss in value is $900.

    b. If defective service was rendered, then loss in value is value of flawless service less value of the defective service. This is a subjective standard (the value is the value to the plaintiff).

2. Other Loss
   Other loss involves two types of damages, incidental and consequential.

    a. Incidental
       Costs incurred in a reasonable attempt to avoid loss, even if unsuccessful.

    b. Consequential
       Costs or injury to persons or property resulting from breach.

3. Cost Avoided
   Savings to the plaintiff from not having to perform further.

4. Loss Avoided
   Any loss avoided by the salvaging or reallocation of resources that would have been devoted to performance of contract.

5. Example
   A contracts to build B a home for $100,000, payable as work progresses. A's cost would be $60,000. A does half the work ($50,000 due) incurring $30,000 in expenses. B refuses to pay. A uses the unused lumber and materials, worth $10,000, on another job. A's loss in value is $100,000 (what is due to him overall less what he has actually received). He has

incurred no other loss. By stopping work midway, A avoids spending an additional $30,000. Therefore, A's expectation damages award is $100,000 - 30,000 - 10,000 = $60,000.

6. Nominal Damages (Rest. 2d. § 346)
When a contract is breached, but plaintiff has not suffered actual damages, a court may grant nominal damages.

B. Promised Performance (Nonmonetary) (Rest. 2d. § 348)
There is difficulty in measuring loss in value when the performance not rendered involves services, e.g., builder refuses to complete work, seller does not deliver goods, etc. In such cases courts utilize one of two measures of damages:

1. Cost of Completing Performance
Damages are awarded in the amount it would cost plaintiff to properly complete the work that the breaching party began.

2. Diminution in Value/"Benefit of the Bargain"
Damages are calculated as the difference between the value of a complete performance and the value of defendant's defective performance.

a. This measure in damages is favored when the cost of completing performance is clearly disproportional to the probable loss in value resulting from the incomplete or defective work. Example: A builds a pool but erroneously uses blue tile instead of green tile. The diminution in the pool's market value is $1, but the cost of properly completing the work is $1,000. It would be economically wasteful to force A to expend $1,000.

b. However, willful breach or public policy may induce a court to award cost of completion damages; such considerations may override economic waste. Example: A knows the pool was supposed to have green tile, but he installs blue tile anyhow because he has too much of it lying around. A may be required to remedy the defective performance or pay for someone else to do it.

C. Specific Examples of Expectation Damages

1. Sale of Goods Contracts

a. Breach by Buyer (remedies of seller) (UCC § 2-703) Mnemonic: **ROW SCRAP**

i. Recover Ordinary contract damages, i.e., contract price less market price plus incidental damages (without reselling the goods).

ii. Withhold delivery of goods.

iii. Stop delivery by bailee or carrier.

iv. Cancel entire contract.

v. Resell All goods and recover any loss from the contract price.

vi. Price of goods that were actually accepted by the buyer is recoverable.

b. Breach by Seller (remedies of buyer) (UCC § 2-711) Mnemonic: **MSG Causes Cancer**

i. Monetary Damages (market price at breach less contract price plus incidental and consequential damages).

ii. Obtain Specific performance.

iii. Recover contracted for Goods (if total or partial payment was made).

iv. Cancel the contract.

v. Cover – buy substitute goods and recover the difference between the contract price and market price.

2. Sale of Land Contracts
Damages are awarded based on the difference between the contract price and the fair market value of the real property at the time of breach.

3. Employment Contracts
In equity, an injunction may be granted. At law:

a. Employer Breaches
Employee recovers full contract price for the remainder of the employment term.

b. Employee Breaches
Employer recovers cost of obtaining a substitute if it is above the contract price. Two types of breaches by employee:

i. Intentional
Employee is barred from recovering expectation damages but may recover restitution in quantum meruit for substantial performance.

ii. Unintentional
Employee is allowed to recover in quasi-contract the value of work done prior to unintentional breach.

4. Construction Contracts

a. Breach by Builder

i. Before Construction Commenced
Owner of the premises can recover excess cost of building above the contract price and the reasonable cost of delays.

ii. During Construction

Cost of completion and reasonable damages for delay.

iii. Late Performance
Subjects builder to liability for damages caused by delay.

iv. A builder can recover in quasi-contract for the value of work done if the breach was unintentional.

b. Breach by Property Owner

i. Before Construction Began
Builder recovers lost profits.

ii. During Construction
Builder recovers lost profits and expenses incurred.

iii. After Construction is Completed
Builder recovers contract price plus interest.

III. LIMITATIONS ON DAMAGES

A. Foreseeability (Rest. 2d. § 351, UCC § 2-715)
Generally applies to consequential and incidental losses. The damages must be foreseeable to the breaching party at the time the contract was made, not at the time of breach. A loss is foreseeable if it naturally follows from the breach or if the breaching party had actual notice that such a loss would result from a breach. (See Hadley v. Baxendale.)

B. Certainty (Rest. 2d. § 352)
A party must establish with reasonable certainty the amount of its loss and the fact that it would have avoided the loss but for the breach. Some types of damages are generally considered to be uncertain, such as lost profits or lost publicity.

C. New-business Rule
Courts are not very receptive to claims for lost profits made by new businesses that have no prior history of profitability. But a

court will consider such claims in light of the plaintiff's experience in the industry and the diligence of his efforts in running the business.

D. Mitigation (Rest. 2d. § 350)

The injured party is not compensated for damages resulting from a breach that the nonbreaching party could have reasonably avoided. Compensation will be granted if an unsuccessful, but reasonable, effort to avoid the loss was made.

1. Comparable Alternatives
   If a comparable opportunity exists, P must accept it and use it to mitigate damages caused by the defendant's breach. If the plaintiff fails to accept a comparable alternative, the court will not award him the damages that could have been avoided. Criteria for comparability includes location, type of services, hours of work, status, etc.

2. Incomparable Alternatives
   The existence of incomparable alternatives will not reduce damages unless they are actually accepted by the plaintiff. Money earned at a new opportunity will be used to mitigate the damage award if the party in breach proves that the plaintiff would not have accepted this opportunity but for the breach. (This is more likely to occur if the contract was for the personal services of the plaintiff). However, if the plaintiff shows that he could have accepted both opportunities, there will be no reduction of damages.

3. The breaching party has the burden of proving that the plaintiff failed to mitigate and that a comparable opportunity existed.

4. UCC: If a seller breaches a sales contract, the buyer must try to "cover" by buying substitute goods. If the buyer breaches, the seller does not have a duty to mitigate. He may choose from a number of remedies.

IV. LIQUIDATED AND NONRECOVERABLE DAMAGES AND PENALTIES

A. Agreed Remedies/Liquidated Damages

In some cases, the parties have included a liquidated-damages clause in their contract. Such a clause provides a remedy, should either party breach the contract. Such agreements take the place of expectation, reliance, restitution, and quasi-contractual remedies.

1. Enforceable if:

   a. Actual damages caused by the breach were difficult to ascertain at the time the contract was executed, and the remedy clause represents a good faith attempt by the parties to provide for the case of breach.

   b. The amount of stipulated or liquidated damages is reasonable as judged either at the time the contract was made or in light of the actual damages incurred (Rest. 2d. § 356; UCC § 2-718). A reasonable clause at the time of contracting is valid even if actual damages turn out to be lower than expected. Some courts will enforce a reasonable clause even if no actual damages occur. Other courts and the Restatement take the opposite view.

2. Unenforceable

   a. Penalties
   Courts are adamantly opposed to any liquidated-damages clauses that are made to penalize a party for not performing. Such clauses typically compensate the nonbreaching party far in excess of any actual damages suffered. However, if a liquidated remedy clause is reasonable, courts will generally not examine the intent of the parties.

   b. Disclaimers

Clauses limiting a party's liability will not be enforced if the amount of liability allowed is unreasonably small given the foreseeable consequences of a breach.

B. Nonrecoverable Damages
Certain types of damages are generally nonrecoverable:
Mnemonic: **APE**

1. Attorney's Fees
Under the American rule, the value of attorney's fees expended as a result of the breach are generally not recoverable. There are a few exceptions:

   a. In certain situations involving class actions.

   b. "Private Attorney General Theory"
   Litigation that involves important public policies.

   c. Abusive Litigation Practices
   If either party maintained an "unfounded claim or defense in bad faith, or for oppressive reasons."

   d. Statutory Exception

2. Punitive Damages (Rest. 2d § 355)
Generally, damages serve a compensatory purpose only. Punitive damages are awarded only in certain situations:

   a. The breaching party acted in a way that is a tort (i.e., gross negligence) for which punitive damages are available.

   b. If an insurance company refuses to give any reason for not honoring an insurance claim (bad-faith breach).

   c. Breach of fiduciary duty.

   d. Fraudulent conduct.

3. Emotional Distress (Rest. 2d. § 353)
Recovery for emotional distress is denied unless the breach causes serious bodily harm or if serious emotional disturbance is a particularly likely result of breaching such a contract. Contracts where emotional distress will be compensated in case of breach include

   a. Breach of contract to marry.

   b. Loss of cherished object. Example: D, film developer, loses P's film covering P's life over many years.

   c. Failure to properly transmit a message concerned with death or illness.

CASE CLIPS

Sullivan v. O'Connor (1973)

Facts: Sullivan sued her surgeon for breach of contract after the plastic surgery he performed on her nose failed to "enhance her beauty and improve her appearance" as expressly promised.
Issue: Does a doctor breach a contract if a medical procedure does not produce the desired results?
Rule: If a doctor expressly promises that a procedure will produce certain results, a patient may recover damages if that promise is not fulfilled.
Note: Because of the fear that patients will elevate a doctor's opinion to a promise, some courts require written proof of the promise. Other courts completely deny recovery in such cases.
Damages are limited to restitution (doctor's fees) and reliance (loss of value of organ operated upon); expectation (increase in value of successful) is denied.

Vitex Mfg. Corp. v. Caribtex Corp. (1967)

Facts: Pursuant to its contract to process wool for Caribtex, Vitex reopened a closed factory, bought chemicals, and hired workers. Caribtex did not supply any wool. Vitex recovered the amount of its

gains prevented minus losses avoided (operating costs). Caribtex claimed that overhead should have been included in costs.
Issue: Is overhead included in costs when calculating lost profits?
Rule: In a claim for lost profits, overhead is not deducted from gross profits as part of the seller's costs. On the contrary, overhead should be considered a loss caused and be added to gains prevented in the calculation of damages.
Note: Overhead includes salaries, property taxes, general administrative expenses, and other costs that are incurred irrespective of any particular contract.

Laredo Hides Co. v. H & H Meat Products Co. (1974)
Facts: H & H breached a contract to sell cattle hides to Laredo. Laredo purchased hides on the open market and sued for the difference in prices.
Issue: If the seller breaches, is a buyer entitled to recover the difference between the cost of "cover" and the contract price?
Rule: When a seller wrongfully breaches a contract, the buyer can "cover" by purchasing the goods elsewhere in good faith and recover the difference between the price of the substituted goods and the contract price. (See UCC § 2-712.)
Note: The buyer is also entitled to incidental and consequential damages.

R.E. Davis Chem. Corp. v. Diasonics, Inc. (1987)
Facts: Davis breached a contract to buy medical equipment from Diasonics. Diasonics eventually sold the equipment to a third party at the same price. Diasonics claimed it was entitled to offset its lost profits against Davis's deposit and return the balance.
Issue: Are damages for lost profits awarded to a seller who later resells the goods to a third party?
Rule: A seller can recover lost profits against a breaching buyer even if the goods were resold at the same price if the seller can prove that, but for the breach, he would have made two sales and both sales would have been profitable.

United States v. Algernon Blair, Inc. (1973)
Facts: After Blair breached by its failure to pay for part of Coastal Steel's (suing under the name of the US) operating costs, Coastal

ceased work and sought restitution for the work performed. Coastal would have lost money if the contract was fully performed.
Issue: Is a party who justifiably stops work under a contract entitled to restitution for work done, if it would have lost money had the contract not been breached?
Rule: A party can recover in *quantum meruit* (what is deserved) for the value of labor and equipment furnished pursuant to a contract that it justifiably breached, irrespective of whether it would have lost money.
Note: A party suffering a loss under a contract will not recover damages in a suit on the contract, but may always forego a suit on the contract and claim only the reasonable value of the performance rendered.

Rockingham County v. Luten Bridge Co. (1929)

Facts: Luten was in the process of building a bridge for Rockingham when it was told to cease construction because of public opposition to the bridge. Luten completed the bridge and sued for the entire contract price.
Issue: Once notified of repudiation, is the nonbreaching party required to cease performance?
Rule: Once a party is notified of repudiation of or refusal to perform a contract, that party may not continue to perform and recover damages based on full performance.

Parker v. Twentieth Century-Fox Film Corp. (1970)

Facts: Shirley MacLaine contracted to star in a musical for Twentieth Century-Fox. Twentieth Century-Fox later canceled the movie and offered MacLaine a starring part in a western for the same amount of money which she refused.
Issue: Must a party mitigate damages by accepting alternate employment?
Rule: A wrongfully discharged employee is entitled to recover the agreed upon compensation less any amount the employer proves the employee has earned or with reasonable effort might have earned from other employment. The employer must show that the other employment was comparable, or substantially similar, to that of which the employee has been deprived.

Note: A female lead in a western drama filmed in Australia is not comparable to a female lead in a song-and-dance production filmed in Los Angeles.

Jacob & Youngs v. Kent (1921)

Facts: Jacob & Youngs, a contractor hired to build a home for Kent, inadvertently installed a different brand of pipes than that specified in the contract. The pipes used were of comparable price and quality to those specified, but Kent refused to pay Jacob & Youngs unless the pipes were replaced.
Issue: What is the measure of damages against a party who inadvertently breaches a contract in a nonmaterial manner?
Rule: When a party inadvertently breaches a contract in a nonmaterial manner the measure of damages will be the difference in value between the specified and the actual performances rather than the cost to correct.

Groves v. John Wunder Co. (1939)

Facts: John Wunder's contract to lease Groves' land permitted the removal of sand and gravel and required that the property be restored to a level grade. Wunder deliberately did not restore the land's grade.
Issue: How are damages assessed when a party's willful breach of contract damaged another's land, but the cost of completion is greater than the value of the land?
Rule: One who wrongfully and willfully breaches a construction contract is liable for the reasonable cost of completing the required work, rather than the value that completion would add to the land (as held in the lower court).

Peevyhouse v. Garland Coal & Mining Co.
(1962) Note Case

Facts: Garland's lease of the Peevyhouse's farm for strip-mining operations obligated Garland to restore the land to its previous condition. Garland refused to restore the land. Although restoration would cost $29,000, the actual value of the land would only rise by $300 after such work.
Issue: Is "cost of completion" or "diminution in value" used to measure damages for breach of a construction obligation in a contract?

Rule: The measure of damages for breach of a construction obligation is ordinarily the reasonable cost of completing the work properly. However, if the obligation is only incidental to the main purpose of the contract (i.e., to lease) and the cost of performing is grossly disproportional to any economic benefit it will yield, then damages are limited to the diminution in value of the property as a result of the breach (i.e., $300) in order to avoid "unreasonable economic waste."

Hadley v. Baxendale (1854)

Facts: A mill operator, forced to shut down after a shaft broke, hired a common carrier to deliver the broken shaft to an engineer for repairs. The carrier negligently delayed delivering the shaft, forcing the mill to shut down longer than expected.
Issue: Is one liable for all consequences resulting from one's breach of contract?
Rule: The amount of damages that is awarded for a breach is limited to those which were fairly and reasonably contemplated by the parties at the time of contracting. Special circumstances must be communicated by the plaintiff to the defendant beforehand.
Note: This landmark case is accepted by all courts and jurisdictions. Although the case mentions that the carrier was notified that the mill was shut down, this fact seems to have been ignored by the court.

Spang Indus. Inc. v. Aetna Cas. & Surety Co. (1975)

Facts: Spang's delay in delivering steel needed to build a bridge forced the contractor to incur additional expenses, because the concrete had to be poured in one day to avoid oncoming freezing temperatures. Spang sued the surety company when the contractor withheld payment of the entire contract as damages. It is common knowledge that construction has to be delayed once the temperature drops significantly.
Issue: Can knowledge of the consequences of a delay in performance be imputed to a breaching party if the consequences were not expressly communicated?
Rule: A party is liable for all direct damages that both parties to the contract, had they been fully informed and given the issue proper attention, would have anticipated as flowing from a breach at the time they made the contract.

Note: The contractor was awarded the value of the additional expenses it incurred.

Fera v. Village Plaza, Inc. (1976)

Facts: Fera leased space in the Fariborn-Village Plaza with the intention of opening a store. Fera sued for lost profits and the deposit after Village Plaza breached the lease by renting to another party. Testimony concerning profitability of stores in the same area or trade was introduced into evidence.
Issue: Are damages for loss of anticipated profits awarded to a new business?
Rule: Damages are awarded for loss of future profits if they are established with reasonable certainty.

Dave Gustafson & Co. v. State (1968) Note Case

Facts: Gustafson surfaced a new state highway paralleling an older road. As provided in the contract, the state withheld $210 per day for sixty-seven days of delay from the $530,000 due on the contract.
Issue: When will a liquidated damages clause be enforced?
Rule: A liquidated damages clause will be enforced if the damages are difficult or impossible to estimate, the parties made a reasonable attempt to fix fair compensation, and the amount stipulated bears a reasonable relation to probable damages.

Lake River Corp. v. Carborundum Co. (1985)

Facts: Lake River contracted to bag and ship "Ferro Carbo" for Carborundum. Because it had to invest in new machinery, Lake River required Carborundum to supply it with at least 22,500 tons of Ferro or pay prevailing rates for the difference between the quantity bagged and the quantity guaranteed. Carborundum failed to ship Lake River the minimum because of falling demand for its product. Lake River sued for the promised money.
Issue: Is a clause providing for a minimum guaranteed quantity a penalty and therefore unenforceable?
Rule: A contractual damages provision is a penalty and unenforceable as such, where it does not reflect an estimate of the actual damages incurred. A minimum guarantee clause penalizes the breaching party based on when the breach occurs rather than on the gravity of the breach. It reflects neither the operating costs saved nor

the actual profit foregone by the nonbreaching party, but simply rewards the nonbreaching party with a windfall.

Note: The court held that Lake River was entitled to the money due on the contract if it had been completed less operating costs saved.

Chapter 6

FINDING THE LAW OF THE CONTRACT

I. PAROL EVIDENCE RULE

The parol evidence rule is substantive law that renders preliminary negotiations, written documents, conversations, and verbal agreements inadmissible at trial because they are merged into and superseded by the subsequent written contract. Even if a court allows such evidence, its veracity still has to be proved to the jury. The rule controls only what type of evidence is allowed, not whether such evidence is credible.

A. Integration
A writing is integrated if it is adopted by the parties as "a final expression of one or more of the terms of an agreement." (Rest. 2d. § 209(1).)

1. A writing is partially integrated if the parties did not intend for it to include all the terms of the agreement.

2. A writing is completely integrated if the parties intended it to include all the terms of the agreement.
(Rest. 2d. § 210(1).)

B. When Parol Evidence is Admissible

1. Evidence of prior agreements or negotiations may supplement a partially integrated agreement, provided this evidence does not contradict a term of the writing.

2. When an agreement is completely integrated, not even evidence of a consistent additional term is admissible to explain or supplement it. (Rest. 2d. § 216.)

3. Some courts treat contemporaneous oral agreements as prior oral agreements. Others assert that the existence of a

contemporaneous oral agreement automatically proves that the writing is only partially integrated.

4. Parol testimony is admissible to prove a condition precedent to the legal effectiveness of a written contract if the condition does not contradict the express terms of such written agreement.

5. Even if the writing is a complete integration, parol evidence is admissible to show fraud, mistake, or duress in the inducement of the contract. Most courts hold that a merger clause should not be held a bar to actions for fraud.

6. Evidence of subsequent oral agreements will not be barred by the parol evidence rule. The rule only applies to agreements made prior to the final contract.

    a. To avoid the admission of this type of evidence, some parties insert no-oral-modification clauses which find statutory support from UCC § 2-209(2).

    b. An attempted oral modification of a contract that contains a no-oral-modification clause is effective as a waiver only if it is reasonably relied upon.

C. The UCC Version

1. A writing intended to be a final expression of an agreement may not be contradicted by evidence of a prior written or oral agreement or of a contemporaneous oral agreement. (UCC § 2-202.)

2. The writing may be explained or supplemented by course of dealing or usage of trade even if it is a complete integration, unless the course of dealing or trade usage is carefully canceled by the contract's terms. (UCC § 2-202(1).)

3. The writing may be explained or supplemented by evidence of consistent additional terms unless the court finds the writing to be complete and exclusive. (UCC § 2-202(2).)

D. Judge Makes All Parol Evidence Decisions (Rest. 2d § 209(2))
There is concern that juries would be more sympathetic to oral testimony and not realize that written evidence is more accurate.

1. Partial v. Complete Integration

a. The strict view asserts that this question should be answered through an examination of the writing only (four-corners approach).

i. According to this view, a clause that states that the writing represents the complete agreement between the parties (merger clause) will usually lead to a determination that the writing is a complete integration, unless it is obviously clear that it is not.

ii. If a writing is seemingly complete on its face, evidence of a prior oral agreement is admissible only if it is one that the parties would not ordinarily be expected to embody in the writing (see *Mitchell v. Lath*).

b. A more permissive approach looks to extrinsic circumstances along with the face of the writing (see *Lee v. Joseph E. Seagram & Sons, Inc.* and *Masterson v. Sine*).

i. The important consideration is the intent of the parties.

ii. A general merger clause is merely evidence of intent.

c. UCC § 2-202, comment 3
Parol evidence of additional terms is not admissible as above unless "the additional terms are such that, if agreed upon, they would certainly have been included in the document."

2. Judges decide whether or not the writing is an integration (i.e., a final expression of accord). Some courts look to the writing; others look to the parties' intent.

3. Judges also determine if the oral additional terms are contradictory or consistent with the writing. The judge must evaluate the oral testimony.

II. INTERPRETING CONTRACT LANGUAGE

In addition to disputes as to whether a term is actually part of a contract, parties may also disagree as to the meaning of those terms that are part of the contract. Difficulties may arise because the parties do not speak the same language or because certain words may have a special "trade meaning" of which one of the parties is not aware.

A. Role of Judge and Jury

1. Although the meaning of language is a question of fact, it has frequently been removed from the jury by calling it a question of law because of a distrust of uneducated and unsophisticated jurors and a desire for uniformity in interpretation.

2. The test of admissibility of extrinsic evidence to explain the meaning of a written instrument is not whether the instrument appears to be plain and unambiguous on its face, but whether the offered evidence is relevant to prove a meaning to which the language of the instrument is reasonably susceptible (*Pacific Gas & Electric Co. v. G.W. Thomas Drayage & Rigging Co.*).

B. The party that seeks to have a contract term interpreted in a narrower sense that is more favorable to him bears a substantial burden of proof. (See *Frigaliment Importing Co. v. B.N.S. Int'l Sales Corp.*)

C. Objective and Subjective Theories of Interpretation

1. Objectivists and subjectivists agree that where the parties have in fact attached different significance to their language, the objective standard should be used in determining the meaning of the language.

2. Objectivists also argue that even where parties have attached the same meaning to their language, an objective standard should determine the meaning, even if it is different from that which the parties intended.

3. In reality, courts allow parol evidence to help them determine the intended meaning of ambiguous words in a written contract.

D. Restatement (Second) § 201

1. Where all parties have attached the same meaning to an agreement or a term, it is interpreted in accordance with that meaning.

2. Where the parties have attached different meanings to an agreement, it is interpreted in accordance with the meaning attached by one of them if at the time the agreement was made that party did not know or have reason to know of any different meaning attached by the other, and the other knew or had reason to know the meaning attached by the first party.

3. There is no binding contract if the parties unknowingly assign different subjective meanings to an important contract term because there was no meeting of the minds. (See *Raffles v. Wichelhaus*; Rest. 2d. § 20.)

E. Rules in Aid of Interpretation

1. Words and conduct are interpreted in light of all the surrounding circumstances. The principal purpose of the

contract is given great weight if it is ascertainable in light of all the circumstances. (Rest. 2d § 202(1).)

2. Maxims, such as "the term is to be strictly construed against the draftsman," can be used.

3. Contracts will be construed to serve the public interest.

   a. An interpretation that gives a reasonable, lawful, and effective meaning to all the terms is preferred to an interpretation that leaves a part of the contract unreasonable, unlawful, or of no effect. (Rest. 2d § 203(a).)

   b. Contracts that restrain trade or land use are narrowly construed.

4. Specific terms and separately negotiated terms are given greater weight than general language and standardized terms, respectively. (Rest. 2d. § 203(c-d).)

5. Interpret terms with the aid of any relevant course of performance, course of dealing, and usage of trade. (Rest. 2d. § 202(5), UCC §§ 1-205, 2-208.)

F. Hierarchy of Extrinsic Aids (Rest. 2d. § 203(b), UCC § 2-208(2))

1. Express Terms
   Look at the contract terms themselves.

2. Course of Performance
   If the contract has been partially performed, the court will consider how the ambiguous terms were treated.

3. Course of Dealing
   If the parties have made other contracts in the past, the court will consider whether similarly ambiguous terms were used and how were they interpreted by the parties.

4. Trade Usage
   Whether the ambiguous or disputed terms have a common interpretation in the specific industry or trade in which the parties are engaged will be considered.

5. These standards are inapplicable if the contract specifically bars their use.

III. FILLING GAPS

How the courts deal with problems that are not addressed by the parties.

A. When the parties to a bargain sufficiently defined to be a contract have not agreed with respect to a term that is essential to a determination of their rights and duties, a term that is reasonable in the circumstances is supplied by the court. (Rest. 2d. § 204.)

   1. The reasonable omitted term may be supplied even if the writing is completely integrated (see parol evidence rule).

   2. Although extrinsic evidence may be inadmissible to supply the omitted term (e.g., the writing is completely integrated), it may be used to determine what is "reasonable."

B. There are many instances where a court will supply omitted terms (see Chapters 8 & 9 for court-implied conditions and extraordinary events that make performance impracticable):

   1. Obligation of Good Faith

      a. Every contract or duty imposes an obligation of good faith in its performance and enforcement. (UCC § 1-203, Rest. 2d. § 205.)

b. Requirements and Output Contracts
There is an obligation of good faith when demanding or tendering requirements or outputs pursuant to the agreement. (UCC § 2-306(1).)

i. This obligation is satisfied if the buyer's demands are in accordance with established courses of performance and dealing between the parties and the established usages of the trade. (See *Eastern Air Lines, Inc. v. Gulf Oil Corp.*)

ii. A requirements or output contract usually does not include an implied obligation to continue the business.

2. Best Efforts

a. A lawful agreement for exclusive dealing, unless otherwise agreed, imposes a return obligation to use best efforts to promote the product. (See *Wood v. Lucy, Lady Duff-Gordon;* UCC § 2-306(2).)

b. A clause requiring "best efforts to maintain a high volume of sales" is annulled by the philosophy that profit motivation should override sales volume in the absence of consideration.

c. A promise to publish implies a good faith effort to promote the book, including a first printing and advertising budget adequate to give the book a reasonable chance of achieving success. However, while publishers must perform honestly, there is no requirement to perform skillfully.

3. Percentage Lease
Rent is fixed as a stated percentage of the lessee's receipts or profits.

a. If based on gross receipts, a conflict is created. The lessor wants the lessee to maximize gross receipts, while the lessee wants to maximize net profits.

b. When no minimum rent is reserved, a percentage lease must be construed as including an implied covenant to continue the business.

c. Such an obligation is not implied if the lessor is protected by a substantial minimum rental provision.

4. Agreements Without End

   a. Employment Contracts
   The majority of states have not implied a duty to terminate employment contracts in good faith.

   b. Franchise Agreements
   There is a three-way division among courts:

      i. Franchisors cannot terminate without cause.

      ii. The franchisor must give reasonable notice of termination.

      iii. Allow the franchisee a reasonable opportunity to avail himself of the primary efforts and expenditures incurred in setting up the franchise.

5. Course of Performance, Course of Dealing, and Trade Usage
Extrinsic evidence relating to the usage of trade and the parties' course of dealing is admissible to supplement an unambiguous and complete written contract as long as it does not contradict the written agreement's express terms. (UCC § 2-202.)

6. UCC Gap-Fillers
   If it has not been agreed upon, courts determine:

   a. Reasonable price terms. (UCC § 2-305(a).)

   b. Place for delivery. (UCC § 2-308.)

   c. Date payment is due. (UCC § 2-310.)

CASE CLIPS

Gianni v. R. Russell & Co. (1924)

Facts: Gianni claimed that, before renewing his lease, he reached an oral agreement to have the exclusive right to sell soft drinks in lieu of the sale of tobacco in R. Russell's building. Gianni sued for breach when another store was permitted to sell soft drinks.
Issue: Is parol evidence allegedly proving the existence of a prior oral agreement admissible to alter the terms of a written agreement?
Rule: If the subject of the alleged oral agreement is embraced by the written contract, the scope of the oral agreement is taken to be covered by the writing, and the written contract is determined to be the entire agreement between the parties.

Masterson v. Sine (1968)

Facts: Masterson sold a ranch to Sine (his sister) with an option reserved to repurchase the property. Masterson's trustee in bankruptcy sought to utilize the option, but Sine attempted to prove that there was a prior oral agreement barring assignment of the option to anyone outside the family.
Issue: When is parol evidence of an oral collateral agreement admissible?
Rule: Evidence of oral collateral agreements are excluded only when the fact finder is likely to be misled. If it appears that the oral collateral agreement might naturally have been made as a separate agreement, proof of the collateral agreement is permitted, but if the additional agreed upon terms logically would have been included in the document, the evidence must be excluded (UCC § 2-202).

Bollinger v. Cent. Pennsylvania Quarry Stripping & Constr. Co. (1967)

Facts: A written agreement allowed Central Pennsylvania to deposit waste on the Bollinger's property. The Bollingers averred that the omission of a clause providing that Central Pennsylvania would cover the waste was a mutual mistake. Central covered the waste initially, but later stopped doing so.
Issue: Will a contract be reformed if part of the agreement was omitted by mutual mistake?
Rule: If the omission of a clause was caused by mutual mistake, a court in equity has the power to reform the written evidence of a contract to make it correspond to the understanding of the parties. Denial by one party that a mistake was made does not prevent a finding of mutual mistake.

Wisconsin Knife Works v. National Metal Crafters (1986)

Facts: Wisconsin's purchase order included a provision that stated that the contract could not be modified without it's agents written assent. When National missed the delivery deadlines, Wisconsin accepted the late shipments and issued a new set of orders. Wisconsin later terminated the contract after National missed more deadlines. National claimed Wisconsin "waived" the written modification requirement by acceptance of late shipments.
Issue: When does a conduct implying assent to modification "operate as a waiver" (UCC § 2-209(4)) despite a clause forbidding modification by other than in writing?
Rule: Implied acceptance of a modification of a contract containing a clause forbidding anything but a written modification is effective as a waiver only when it is reasonably relied upon by the party seeking to enforce the modification.

Frigaliment Imp. Co. v. B.N.S. Int'l Sales Corp. (1960)

Facts: Frigaliment rejected International's delivery of "stewing chickens" because it said that the contract called for "young chickens." International defended that the contract allowed for it to deliver "any bird of that genus," and that it's prices were too low to suggest that it was selling "broilers."
Issue: How does the court determine the meaning of an ambiguous contract term?

Rule: The party who seeks to have a contract term interpreted in a narrower sense that is more favorable to him bears the substantial burden of persuading the court. In order to determine the meaning of an ambiguous term, the court looks to the contract language, prevalence and actual knowledge of the trade usage, and the dealings between the parties.

Raffles v. Wichelhaus (1864)

Facts: The contract stated that the plaintiff was to deliver the goods on the ship "Peerless." Unknown to both parties there were two different ships bearing the same name but sailing at different times. The defendant refused the plaintiff's goods because he expected the delivery to be made on the "Peerless" which sailed earlier.
Issue: Is there a contract if each party gives a different meaning to a material ambiguity in the contract?
Rule: There is no binding contract if the parties unknowingly assign different meanings to an important contract term. Parol evidence may be given to prove that the parties attributed different meanings to a term.

Oswald v. Allen (1969) Note Case

Facts: Oswald, a Swiss coin collector, offered to buy a collection of Swiss coins from Allen. Allen understood him to mean he wished to buy her "Swiss Coin Collection" which did not include certain Swiss coins in her possession. Oswald, believing he had bought all her Swiss coins, sued for specific performance when she refused to deliver them.
Issue: Does a contract exist when two parties materially differ in their understanding of the object of the contract?
Rule: When terms used to express an agreement are ambivalent, and the parties understand them in different ways, no contract exists unless one party should have been aware of the other's understanding. Such an agreement provides "no sensible basis for choosing between conflicting understandings."

Pacific Gas & Elec. Co. v. G.W. Drayage & Rigging Co. (1968)

Facts: The contract to repair the plaintiff's steam turbine contained an indemnity clause requiring the defendant to pay for all property damage arising out of performance of the contract. When the

defendant damaged the exposed rotor of a turbine, the plaintiff sued. The defendant sought to introduce extrinsic evidence to show that the indemnity clause only held the defendant liable for injury to the property of third parties, not to that of the plaintiff.
Issue: Is evidence of the parties' intention admissible to help explain the meaning of a written instrument?
Rule: Extrinsic evidence of parties' intention is admissible when relevant to prove a meaning to which the language of a written instrument is reasonably susceptible. Even when the meaning of the instrument appears plain and unambiguous on its face, extrinsic evidence having the above effect is admissible.

Steuart v. McChesney (1982)

Facts: The Steuarts granted the McChesneys a right of first refusal, or the right to make a bid if the Steuarts found a purchaser for a parcel of farmland. The property was appraised at $50,000, and the defendants received offers of over $30,000. However, the plaintiffs sought to exercise their right for $7,820, twice the value listed on the tax rolls maintained in the county. The contract provided that county records were to be the source of the McChesneys' offer.
Issue: When an agreement's meaning is clear and unambiguous and yet produces an inequitable result, can extrinsic evidence be introduced to supply another meaning?
Rule: The plain meaning of an unambiguous contract will be enforced despite inequitable results. Plain meaning cannot be distorted to produce ambiguity simply because fairness might warrant a different outcome.

Hurst v. W.J. Lake & Co. (1932) Note Case

Facts: A contract for horse meat specified that meat under the minimum fifty percent protein would be subject to a discount of five dollars. Lake took a discount on meat ranging from 49.53% to 49.96%. In the suit to recover the discount, Hurst offered to prove that trade usage of these terms required a buyer to pay full price for meat consisting of 49.5% protein or more.
Issue: Is evidence of trade usage admissible to demonstrate a meaning other than an unambiguous common meaning of a contract term?

Rule: Trade usage of contract terms may be admitted to show the meaning that the parties intended to impute to a term. Otherwise, the language will be stripped of the meaning that the parties intended to give to it.

Eastern Airlines v. Gulf Oil Corp. (1975)

Facts: Pursuant to its requirements contract to buy fuel from Gulf, Eastern refueled its planes at the least expensive locations only. In response, Gulf breached the contract. Eastern offered proof that minimizing fuel costs by "fuel freighting" was a common industry practice that had been regularly used in previous dealings between the parties.
Issue: Has a buyer met the obligation of good faith in a requirements contract if it has acted according to established courses of industry standards?
Rule: The obligation of good faith in requirements contracts imposed by UCC § 2-306(1) is satisfied if the buyer's conduct concurs with established courses of performance and dealing between the parties and the established usages of the trade.

Wood v. Lucy, Lady Duff-Gordon (1917)

Facts: Lady Duff-Gordon, a famous designer, agreed with Wood that he would have exclusive agency to place her endorsements on clothing designs, to place her designs on sale and to license others to market them. In exchange, Wood promised to keep the books and to split the profits evenly with Duff-Gordon. Duff-Gordon breached by endorsing designs herself and keeping the profits. In defense, she claimed that Wood's promise was illusory, as she had granted him exclusive agency, but he was not obligated to find designs or to sell her labels.
Issue: Is a contract void for lack of mutuality because one party did not promise to use reasonable efforts to perform his duties?
Rule: A promise to use reasonable efforts can be implied from a contract and, therefore, a contract does not fail for lack of mutuality because it does not contain explicit clauses requiring good faith efforts (UCC § 2-306(2)).

Dickey v. Philadelphia Minit-Man Corp. (1954)

Facts: Dickey leased land to Minit-Man for washing, simonizing and polishing cars "and for no other purpose." The lease required the

defendant to pay a percentage of gross sales in addition to a minimum rent. Dickey sued to recover possession after Minit-Man discontinued only the car washing aspect of the business.
Issue: When the amount of rent to be paid is based upon the lessee's gross sales, is there an implied obligation to continue the business on the premises to the fullest extent reasonably possible?
Rule: There is no implied obligation in a percentage sales lease to continue business to the fullest extent because such an implication is vague, uncertain, and generally impracticable. The basis for rejecting an implied obligation is strengthened if the lessor is guaranteed a substantial minimum rent.

Nicholson v. United Pacific Insurance Co. (1985) Note Case
Facts: Nicholson, an owner of an office building, attempted to renovate the building to the satisfaction of his new lessees, UPI. UPI placed several obstacles in the way of completion, and ultimately called Nicholson in breach due to unsatisfactory performance. It was revealed that UPI was attempting to escape the lease agreement. Finding that UPI breached the implied covenant of good faith and fair dealing, the jury awarded compensatory and punitive damages.
Issue: When will the implied covenant of good faith and fair dealing be invoked in a contract between parties of equal bargaining power?
Rule: The tort of breach of the implied covenant of good faith and fair dealing will be committed when a party acts arbitrarily, capriciously or unreasonably.
Note: While the tort was once reserved to contracts between parties of unequal bargaining power where the stronger party has taken advantage of its position, some jurisdictions have extended it, as in this case, to contracts where a party's misconduct alone warrants use of the doctrine.

Bloor v. Falstaff Brewing Corp. (1979)
Facts: Falstaff bought the Ballantine brewing labels, trademarks, etc., from Bloor for a set price plus a royalty on each barrel of the Ballantine beer sold. Falstaff allowed sales of Ballantine beer to fall in the interest of increasing profits. A clause in their contract required Falstaff to use its "best efforts to promote and maintain a high volume of sales. . . ."

Issue: Is a "high volume of sales" clause breached by an emphasis on profits without regard to the effect on sales volume?
Rule: Although a party is not required to spend itself into bankruptcy, a clause requiring "best efforts to maintain a high volume of sales" for a specified product is violated by a philosophy that emphasizes profit without fair consideration of the effect on the sales volume.

Zilg v. Prentice-Hall, Inc. (1983)

Facts: P-H, a publisher, was given contractual discretion in marketing its publication of Zilg's book. After deciding that Zilg's Marxist-leaning book would have limited popularity, P-H revised its initial marketing budget figures downward. Zilg sued, claiming P-H did not use its best efforts to promote his book.
Issue: To what extent does discretion to tailor promotion efforts to a product's likely market limit the implied responsibility to use best efforts to promote a product?
Rule: A promise to promote implies a good faith effort to do so, including an initial production and advertising budget adequate to give the product a reasonable chance of achieving success. Once this initial obligation is fulfilled, only good faith business judgment is required if the contract contains a clause giving the producer/ promoter discretion over marketing efforts.

Doubleday & Co., Inc., v. Curtis (1985) Note Case

Facts: The actor Tony Curtis made a two-novel contract with Doubleday. When his second novel encountered unfavorable reviews with his Doubleday editor, he refused to incorporate changes, accept editing help or send the novel to a "novel doctor." Doubleday terminated the contract pursuant to the condition that the novel must be "satisfactory to Publisher. . . ."
Issue: If a contract contains a condition of satisfaction and implies that the producer will help the creator to meet this condition, what are the limitations on the producer's right to terminate for dissatisfaction?
Rule: A producer may, in its discretion, terminate a production contract, provided that the termination is made in good faith and the failure of the creator to submit a satisfactory product was not caused by the bad faith of the producer.

Bak-A-Lum Corp. of America v. ALCOA Bldg. Prod. Inc. (1976)

Facts: ALCOA terminated an exclusive distributorship with BAL having instigated a major expansion of BAL's facilities at substantial cost.

Issue: Must a franchisor disclose its intention to terminate an agreement when it knows the franchisee will incur substantial costs in fulfillment of the agreement?

Rule: There is an implied covenant of good faith and fair dealing in franchise agreements requiring reasonable notice of termination, reasonableness to be considered under all the circumstances, so as not to impair the right of the franchisee to the fruits of the contract.

Lockewill, Inc. v. United States Shoe Corp. (1977) Note Case

Facts: The plaintiff operated a successful exclusive distributorship of Pappagallo shoes in the St. Louis area for years under an oral agreement with the former owner of Pappagallo. When the business was sold, US Shoe, the new owner, refused to honor the oral agreement which had no provisions for termination or duration.

Issue: What obligation does the grantor of an indefinite exclusive agency have to the grantee or agent?

Rule: The recipient of an exclusive agency must be allowed a reasonable time to recoup the investment pursuant to the agreement. However, after such reasonable time has passed, the grantor has the right to terminate either the agreement or the exclusivity of it. Formal notice is not required if the contract does not provide for it.

Nanakuli Paving & Rock Co. v. Shell Oil Co., Inc. (1981)

Facts: Nanakuli entered into a long-term contract to buy asphalt from Shell. Although not explicitly required to, Shell gave Nanakuli price protection for five years in accordance with industry-wide custom in Hawaii. Due to rising costs, Shell raised its prices.

Issue: Will trade usage that is reinforced by the course of dealings between the parties be incorporated into an agreement?

Rule: A course of dealings that complies with a prevalent trade usage of which the parties are or should be aware will be incorporated into an agreement provided it is consistent with the express terms of the contract.

Columbia Nitrogen Corp. v. Royster Co. (1971)

Facts: Columbia contracted to purchase a minimum of 31,000 tons of phosphate each year for three years from Royster. The contract set the price per ton, subject to an escalation clause based on production costs. Because phosphate prices tumbled, Columbia could not resell it at a competitive price and consequently ordered less than a tenth of the contract amount in the first year. Columbia sought to introduce evidence that, despite the express terms of the contract, contracts of this type were meant to be mere projections of price and quantity.

Issue: May parol evidence pertaining to the usage of the trade and the parties' course of dealing be admitted when the terms of the written agreement are unambiguous?

Rule: Even when an agreement is unambiguous, extrinsic evidence about the usage of trade and the parties' course of dealing is admissible.

Note: Such parol evidence should be excluded when it cannot be reasonably construed as consistent with the terms of the contract, but it may be introduced even when the writing was intended to be a complete statement of the terms of the agreement.

Chapter 7

PERFORMANCE AND BREACH

I. CONDITIONS

A condition is an *event*, not certain to occur, which must occur, unless its nonoccurrence is excused, before performance under a contract becomes due (Rest. 2d. § 224). Failure to perform a condition discharges the other party's duty to perform. Example: B promises to pay A on the condition that A delivers the goods by a certain date. B does not have to pay if A does not make delivery in time: the condition fails.

II. CATEGORIZATION OF CONDITIONS ACCORDING TO TIME

A. Condition Concurrent
The parties are bound to perform at the same time so that the performance of each one is dependent on the simultaneous performance of the other. Example: B hands cash to C with one hand and takes goods with the other.

B. Condition Precedent
An event, other than a lapse of time, must occur before the other party has an absolute duty of performance. Example: A must deliver the goods before B has a duty to pay.

C. Condition Subsequent
An event discharges an already existing absolute duty of performance (very rare).

D. Precedent v. Subsequent

1. No Substantive Difference

2. Procedural Difference

    a. The party to whom the duty is owed must prove that a condition precedent has occurred.

b. The party who owes the duty must prove that the condition subsequent has occurred.

3. The Restatement (Second) does not distinguish between conditions subsequent and precedent.

III. EXPRESS CONDITIONS

Parties can expressly agree that some event must occur before a party's duty to perform arises.

A. Strict Compliance Required

Usually, all of the requirements of the express condition must be met before a duty to render the dependent performance arises. For example, if a contract for the sale of a car requires that a down payment be made by a specific date as a condition of delivery, late payment discharges the duty to deliver.

1. Courts try to avoid forfeiture and may excuse the nonoccurrence of a condition if it is not a material part of the exchange. (Rest. 2d. § 229.)

2. Courts may not strictly enforce a condition if substantial performance can be proved.

3. To determining whether a contract contains an express condition, court looks at:

   a. Language
   Words such as "provided that," "when," "as soon as," and "after" all suggest that a condition exists.

   b. Intent of the Parties
   Intent of the parties is determined by looking at the contract, circumstances surrounding its formation, and the parties' conduct subsequent to its formation.

   c. Control

If occurrence of the event is within the control of one of the parties, it is more likely to be a condition.

4. Conditions of Satisfaction
An agreement can make a party's performance conditional upon his satisfaction with the other party's performance.

   a. Objective standard of reasonableness is used where the condition calls for satisfaction as to commercial value or quality, operative fitness, or mechanical utility.

   b. Subjective satisfaction is required where the condition involves fancy, taste, or judgment (dissatisfaction can be unreasonable as long as it is in good faith).

   c. Satisfaction of an Independent Party

      i. Example: A party's duty to pay can be conditioned upon an architect's subjective approval of the builder's performance.

      ii. Majority Rule
      To suspend a third party's approval as a condition, it must be demonstrated that the refusal was made in bad faith, not that approval was unreasonably or unfairly withheld.

      iii. Minority Rule
      An unreasonable refusal is sufficient to excuse a third party's approval as a condition to payment.

IV. CONSTRUCTIVE CONDITIONS

In the interest of fairness a court will sometimes imply certain events (performances) to be conditions that must be fulfilled prior to the rendering of future performance. That is the case, for example, when the parties have agreed to what duties are expected of each other but have not provided a sequence of performance for those duties. Example: A agrees to pay B and B agrees to build A's house, but there is no payment schedule.

A. A party's performance is a constructive condition to the performance of the other party's stated subsequent duties.

B. Order of Performance not Agreed Upon:

1. If exchange of performances can be rendered simultaneously, then courts view the performances as constructive concurrent conditions, i.e., conditions precedent to each other, and both must be performed simultaneously. (Rest. 2d. § 234(1).)

2. If the performance of one party requires a longer period of time, his performance is usually due first and is a constructive condition precedent to the other's performance. (Rest. 2d. § 234(2).)

3. Where a contract is made to perform work and no agreement is made as to time of payment, the work must be substantially performed before payment can be demanded.

C. Bilateral Contracts

The modern rule is that there is a presumption that mutual promises in a contract are dependent and are to be so regarded whenever possible.

V. EXCUSE OF A CONDITION

If a condition to a party's performance has not been satisfied, that party is discharged from having to perform, unless the nonoccurrence is legally excused.

A. Nonmaterial Breach

The constructive condition that full performance must be rendered before the other party is required to perform is excused where the party rendering incomplete performance has only committed a nonmaterial breach. Example: A paid B $499.

The contract price was $500. The "injured" party has to perform, but can recover any damages caused by the breach.

B. Material Breach
If there is a material breach, the breaching party has failed to fulfill the constructive condition of full performance. The "injured" party's duties do not arise, and he is discharged from having to perform. He has the option to repudiate the contract.

1. Factors Determining Materiality of Breach (Rest. 2d. § 241)

   a. The extent to which the injured party will be deprived of benefit expected

   b. The adequacy of damages

   c. The extent to which the breaching party would suffer forfeiture

   d. Likelihood failure will be cured

   e. Whether the breaching party's behavior comported with good faith and fair dealing

2. If a party repudiates a contract, claiming failure of a condition which is later excused, he will have materially breached.

   a. As a caution, an injured party can request an assurance of due performance if there are reasonable grounds for insecurity. (UCC § 2-609; Rest. 2d. § 251.)

   b. Although a party has no right to refuse performance of one contract because the other party has breached a separate contract between them, such a situation may give rise to justifiable grounds for insecurity.

C. Doctrine of Substantial Performance
Primarily applied to building contracts, this excuses the condition of complete performance if the work is substantially performed.

1. The test is whether the breach was material or not (see above for factors).

2. If a breach was minor and there was substantial performance, the injured party has a claim for damages but must perform its obligations.

3. The rule prevents forfeiture where a breach is minor.

4. It is applied mostly to constructive conditions.

5. UCC § 2-601
   Under the UCC, if the goods in a sale-of-goods contract are defective "in any respect," the buyer is entitled to reject the entire shipment, reject only the defective goods, or accept the whole. Courts have often applied the doctrine of substantial performance to limit a buyer's right to rejection.

   a. The parties can "otherwise agree," i.e., provide an arrangement other than rejection for defective goods.

   b. The buyer cannot reject goods under an installment contract unless the flaw substantially impairs the value of that installment or of the whole contract. (UCC § 2-612.)

   c. Rejection by the buyer must take place "within a reasonable time." (UCC § 2-602(1).)

   d. After the buyer has accepted under UCC § 2-606:

      i. There is no right of rejection.

      ii. Revocation of the acceptance is valid only if the nonconformity substantially impairs the value of the goods to him and takes place within a reasonable time. (UCC § 2-608.)

e. If the goods were rejected and the time for performance has not expired, the seller may cure the defect. (UCC § 2-508.)

D. Promise v. Condition

1. The performance of a party can be construed as either a condition, which must be fulfilled before the other has to perform, or as an absolute obligation (promise), which is not a condition to future performance. Due to the harshness of forfeiture, courts sometimes interpret express conditions to be promises in cases where a nonmaterial deviation from the required performance occurs. Example: B contracts to design C's home and to secure city's approval of the plans. B does the work, but the city does not grant approval. To avoid forfeiture, courts may rule that B's obligation to secure the city's approval was a promise and not a condition for payment. Of course, C is entitled to damages for breach.

2. Courts look to the intent of the parties to determine if the contract language is a promise or a condition.

3. The language of the contract will be interpreted as a promise to avoid forfeiture in some cases. (See *Jacob & Young v. Kent.*)

4. Conditions with an Implied Promise
A contract term may be both a condition and a promise for one party.

a. A condition within control of the party may carry an implied promise of "best efforts" to perform the condition. Example: B promises to buy C's home, if he can obtain financing. B must make "best efforts" to obtain financing. Where a conditional promise is not performed, the other party is entitled to suspend performance and sue for damages.

b. Order of Preferences

The order of preference in interpreting nonperformance is first as a promise, then as a condition, and if the other two are not possible, as a promissory condition. (Rest. 2d. § 227.)

E. Divisible Contracts
It is not a condition precedent to the other party's performance that all segments of a divisible contract be performed.

1. If the part to be performed by one party consists of several distinct items, and the price to be paid by the other is apportioned to each item to be performed, such contract will generally be held to be divisible.

2. If a party performs a segment of a divisible contract, he is entitled to the other party's equivalent performance for the completed segment. (Rest. 2d. § 240.)

F. Anticipatory Repudiation
An anticipatory repudiation occurs when a party clearly indicates that he will not render future performance when it becomes due. Example: A contracts to sell wheat to B in November. In July, A informs B that he will not deliver the wheat. There is a requirement that the threatened future breach be total or material for the nonrepudiating party to be excused from rendering performance.

1. The nonrepudiating party is, therefore, excused from performing the constructive condition of manifesting a prospective ability and willingness to perform.

2. The nonrepudiating party is entitled not only to suspend his performance, but to cancel the contract and immediately sue for damages. (Rest. 2d. § 253; UCC § 2-610.)

3. The doctrine of anticipatory breach has not ordinarily been extended to unilateral contracts. Even if the party repudiates an installment contract, each delinquent installment must be sued upon after it becomes due.

4. Repudiation may be retracted prior to any material change of position by the other party in reliance on the repudiation. (Rest. 2d. § 256(1); UCC § 2-611.)

5. If a party's conduct indicates an inability to perform, the nonrepudiating party may suspend performance and request an adequate assurance of performance. Failure to give assurance within thirty days (UCC) or within a reasonable time may be treated as a repudiation. (Rest. 2d. § 251; UCC § 2-609(1).)

6. UCC Damages for Seller's Repudiation:

   a. UCC § 2-713(1) states that damages are measured from the time the buyer learns of breach by the seller.

   b. This section is modified by § 2-610(a), which states that the nonrepudiating party may await performance for a commercially reasonable time.

G. Prevention of Performance

The nonoccurrence of a condition will be excused if the conduct of the party benefitting from the condition prevents the occurrence of the condition.

1. The test is whether the party being prevented from performing the condition assumed the risk of the preventing party's conduct.

2. Making performance more difficult, but not impossible, will not necessarily excuse the condition.

3. In every contract there is a constructive condition of cooperation. (Rest. 2d. § 205.)

H. Waiver of a Condition

1. Which Conditions May Be Waived

a. A party may waive performance of a condition inserted for his benefit.

b. A party cannot, by waiver of a condition precedent to his own liability, create an obligation where none previously existed, unless consideration is given for the waiver.

c. Material conditions cannot be waived.

2. Types of Waiver

a. Estoppel Waiver
Estoppel Waiver is binding if manifestation of waiver of a condition, before it was to happen, is materially relied upon by the other party. However, a waiver can be retracted if no reliance occurred.

b. Election Waiver
Election Waiver is binding if a party decides to continue under the contract after a condition has not been performed.

3. After waiving a condition, a party still has a right to damages.

I. Restitution for a Defaulting Plaintiff
In equity, an injunction may be granted. At law:

1. Employee Breaches of an Employment Contract
Employee is barred from recovering expectation damages but may recover restitution in quantum meruit.

2. A party may recover restitution damages for the reasonable value of work completed.

CASE CLIPS

Luttinger v. Rosen (1972)

Facts: Luttinger agreed to buy a home from Rosen subject to the express condition that Luttinger obtained mortgage financing at a stipulated interest rate. Luttinger was only able to get financing at a higher rate and refused to go through with the purchase even though Rosen offered to change the terms of the contract. Luttinger sued for the return of the deposit.

Issue: Is a contract unenforceable if a condition precedent is not fulfilled?

Rule: If a condition precedent is not fulfilled, the contract is not enforceable. Any offer to alter the express condition to enable the parties to comply with its terms may be rejected.

Mattei v. Hopper (1958)

Facts: Mattei agreed to buy property from Hopper. The agreement called for a $1,000 down payment and the balance to be paid within 120 days subject to Mattei obtaining satisfactory leases. Hopper refused to complete the sale, claiming Mattei's promise was illusory because he was not actually bound: Hopper was obligated to sell, but Mattei only had to buy if he was satisfied with the leases.

Issue: Does a contract lack consideration if the assent of one party to the agreement is conditioned by a satisfaction clause?

Rule: An agreement that contains a satisfaction clause is not illusory (lacking consideration or mutuality of obligation) if performance of the condition can be judged by a reasonable person standard or the party subject to the satisfaction clause acts in good faith.

Gibson v. Cranage (1878)

Facts: Gibson expressly agreed to the condition that Cranage must be personally satisfied with his portrait of Cranage's deceased daughter before being required to pay. Cranage was dissatisfied and refused to pay.

Issue: Is a contract term requiring personal satisfaction an enforceable condition?

Rule: If a contract's express terms provide that a party is to be personally satisfied before having to perform his part of the contract, that party may insist upon his right as given him by the contract. However, the dissatisfaction must be in good faith.

Second Nat'l Bank v. Pan-American Bridge Co. (1910)

Facts: Payment by Second National Bank was conditioned on its architect's approval of Pan-American's plans. After construction of the originally approved plans reached the sixth floor, the architect changed his mind and insisted that Pan-American replace the connection rivets for beams and columns with sturdier connections. On Pan-American's refusal, Second National made the replacements and deducted the cost from Pan-American's payment.

Issue: Will unreasonable and unfair conduct excuse the condition of obtaining approval prior to payment?

Rule: Approval as a condition precedent to payment is enforceable unless a party demonstrates bad faith. A claim that the approval was unreasonably and unfairly withheld is insufficient to constitute bad faith.

Peacock Constr. Co. v. Modern Air Conditioning, Inc. (1977)

Facts: Payment by Peacock, a contractor, to the subcontractor, Modern Air Conditioning, was to be made "within 30 days after the completion of the work . . . and full payment thereof by the owner." Peacock claimed that payment by the owner was a condition precedent to paying.

Issue: Can the risk of payment failure by the owner be shifted to the subcontractor by an ambiguous contract provision?

Rule: Payment by the owner to the general contractor is not a condition precedent to the general contractor's duty to pay the subcontractors unless the contract clearly expresses this intention.

Note: A contract dispute concerning the intentions of the parties will be interpreted as a matter of law by the court when the contract involves a general contractor and small subcontractors on a construction job.

Mascioni v. I.B. Miller, Inc. (1933) Note Case

Facts: I.B. Miller, a contractor, was to make payments to his subcontractor Mascioni "as received from the owner." Mascioni brought suit to recover payments even though the owner had not paid I.B. Miller. I.B. Miller introduced extrinsic evidence to show that payment by the owner was a condition to payment to the subcontractor.

Issue: Can the risk of payment failure by the owner be shifted to the subcontractor by an ambiguous contract provision?

Rule: A promise to pay a debt upon the happening of a certain condition can be a condition precedent that the debt shall not be paid until the condition is satisfied.

Note: This rule contradicts the *Peacock* rule but may be distinguishable because here there was extrinsic evidence indicating that the parties intended for the subcontractor to assume the risk of the owners' nonpayment.

Hicks v. Bush (1962)

Facts: Hicks and Bush contracted to combine their business interests to effect a more efficient operation. Hicks performed his obligations, but Bush did not. Bush sought to introduce evidence that the parties had made a contemporaneous oral agreement stipulating that the contract would only be binding if they obtained financing, which was not forthcoming. The writing was silent on this issue.

Issue: Is parol testimony admissible to prove the existence of a condition precedent to a written agreement?

Rule: Parol testimony is admissible to prove a condition precedent to the legal effectiveness of a written agreement if the condition does not contradict the express terms of such written agreement "in a real sense."

Kingston v. Preston (1773)

Facts: Preston promised to sell his business to Kingston, and Kingston promised to post a bond as security guaranteeing his payment. When he did not give security, Preston refused to sell. Kingston sued for breach, claiming that his promise was not a condition to the defendant's duty to sell.

Issue: When each party to a contract makes an interdependent promise to the other, may a party sue for breach without having substantially performed on its promise?

Rule: When parties exchange promises which are mutually dependent, each party's substantial performance of its promise is a constructive condition to the other party's performance of any subsequent duties.

Hanks v. GAB Business Services, Inc., (1982) Note Case

Facts: GAB agreed to purchase Hanks' business under terms which called for yearly installment payments. Hanks agreed not to compete with GAB for five years but he did not abide by this term. GAB sought to enjoin the Hanks' breach. When the next installment payment became due, Hanks counterclaimed for the amount.

Issue: May a party recover damages for breach when it has not substantially performed on its own promise?

Rule: A promise may be regarded as independent of the other party's promise when it only goes to part of the consideration on both sides for a larger agreement.

Note: A party may recover without substantial performance of its own promise if it is independent of the other party's promise.

Walker & Co. v. Harrison (1957)

Facts: Harrison rented a neon sign from Walker & Co. The contract provided that Walker & Co. was to maintain the sign. Harrison repudiated the agreement after the company failed to clean graffiti and tomatoes from it.

Issue: May a party repudiate his contractual duties if the other party has committed only a minor breach of his obligations?

Rule: A party must prove that the other party committed a material breach of the contract before the contract can be repudiated. Repudiation is "fraught with peril," for should the court not find that the other party materially breached the contract, the repudiator himself will have been guilty of material breach.

Stewart v. Newbury (1917)

Facts: Although a contract for excavation work did not specify the terms and conditions regarding time or manner of payment, Stewart alleged that payment was to be made in "the usual manner" (85 percent every 30 days). After Newbury refused to pay, Stewart asserted he was excused from completely performing the contract.

Issue: May a party discontinue performance and demand payment without having substantially performed?

Rule: Where a contract is made to perform work and no agreement is made as to time of payment, the work must be substantially performed before payment can be demanded.

Kanavos v. Hancock Bank & Trust Co. (1985)

Facts: Kanavos contracted to acquire the right of first refusal to buy stock from Hancock Bank. The bank later sold the stock to a third party without giving Kanavos an opportunity to exercise his right.
Issue: In a contract which calls for concurrent performances, when is a repudiating party liable for its breach?
Rule: For a repudiating party to be liable for breach of a contract that calls for concurrent performances, the nonrepudiating party must prove that it had the capability to satisfy its contractual obligations.

Jacob & Youngs v. Kent (1921)

Facts: Jacob & Youngs, a contractor hired to build a home for Kent, inadvertently installed a different brand of pipes than that specified in the contract. The pipes used were of comparable price and quality to those specified, but Kent refused to pay Jacob & Youngs unless the pipes were replaced.
Issue: Is a party who inadvertently breaches a contract in a nonmaterial and insignificant manner liable for breach?
Rule: Considerations of both justice and the intentions of the parties will allow the court to characterize some promises as merely independent and insignificant promises allowing only nominal damages as opposed to treating such promises as conditions of the contract.

Plante v. Jacobs (1960)

Facts: Plante contracted to build a home for Jacobs who later refused to continue payment because of defects in the construction. Plante did not complete the house and sued for the unpaid balance. Jacobs claimed that Plante failed to substantially perform. The market value of the house was not significantly affected by the defects.
Issue: Is a contractor liable for failure to substantially perform if there are construction defects that do not significantly affect market value?
Rule: The test for substantial performance is whether the performance meets the essential purpose of the contract. As applied to construction of a house, substantial performance does not mean that every detail must be in strict compliance with the specifications and the plans. Contract recovery will be diminished by the *cost of replacement rule* for small defects, and by the *diminished value rule* to

avoid unreasonable economic waste, in cases of defects whose correction is expensive but adds little or nothing to the value.

United States v. Spearin (1918)

Facts: Spearin agreed to build a dry dock for the U.S. government. Part of the work required rebuilding the sewer system. When a dam in the sewer system, which did not appear in the plans and specifications provided by the government, flooded the excavation site, Spearin stopped work and the government subsequently annulled the contract.
Issue: Is a contractor responsible for the consequences of defects in the plans and specifications prepared by the owner?
Rule: If the contractor is bound to build according to specifications prepared by the owner, the contractor will not be responsible for the consequences of defects in the specifications. This implied warranty is not overcome by general clauses requiring the contractor to examine the site and to assume responsibility for the work.

Stees v. Leonard (1874)

Facts: Leonard, following all of the plans and specifications in the contract, tried unsuccessfully twice to construct a building. Leonard sought to be excused from performance because the land was composed of quicksand.
Issue: If confronted with an unforseen impediment, is a contractor excused from performing his obligations?
Rule: If a party binds himself, by a positive, express contract, to do an act in itself possible, performance is required unless is it rendered impossible by an act of God, the law, or the other party to the contract.

Internatio-Rotterdam, Inc. v. River Brand Rice Mills, Inc. (1958)

Facts: A contract for the sale of rice required shipment by the end of December with at least two weeks notice to the shipper, River Brand Rice. The shipper canceled the contract after Internatio-Rotterdam failed to give notice by December 17. The buyer's letters of credit only guaranteed payment for a December delivery.
Issue: May a party cancel a contract upon the nonoccurrence of a condition precedent in a sale of goods contract?

Rule: If a provision "goes to the essence" of a sale of goods contract, it can serve as a condition precedent to delivery, the nonoccurrence of which entitles the seller to rescind the contract even if the buyer later performs.

Hays Merchandise, Inc. v. Dewey (1970)

Facts: Dewey received less than half of the stuffed animals he ordered. After an exasperated Dewey said he did not want the remainder of the stuffed animals, another shipment arrived. He was told he could return them but instead put them on display for sale during the Christmas season. Several months later, Dewey shipped a considerable amount of toys back to Hays Merchandise, who refused to accept them. Hays Merchandise sued when it was not paid for the toys.

Issue: Is a revocation of acceptance effective if the nonconformity does not substantially impair the value to the party and the notice of revocation took place several months after delivery?

Rule: An effective revocation of acceptance requires that (1) a nonconformity substantially impairs its value to the party and (2) the notice of the revocation takes place within a reasonable time (UCC § 2-608).

Gill v. Johnstown Lumber Co. (1892)

Facts: As a result of a flood, Gill was only able to drive and deliver part of the four million feet of logs specified in a contract. The contract provided that Gill be paid set prices per thousand feet of logs delivered, depending on the type of log. Johnstown claimed that since not all the logs were delivered, it was not obligated to pay.

Issue: Is there a divisible contract if the work undertaken consists of several items and the consideration to be paid is apportioned among the several items?

Rule: A contract will generally be held severable if the part to be performed by one party consists of several distinct items, and the price to be paid by the other is either apportioned to each item to be performed or left to be implied by law.

Pennsylvania Exchange Bank v. United States (1959) Note Case

Facts: The United States Army Signals Corps contracted to pay Joseph Lerner & Sons to equip itself for the production of "microwave magic tees." The work was to be done in a four step process of which Joseph Lerner & Sons had completed three before assigning all of its assets to a creditor, to avoid bankruptcy. An assignee, Pennsylvania Bank sued for the remaining amount owed by the government on the first three stages.

Issue: Is a contract divisible when its stages are merely incidental to an ultimate objective?

Rule: A contract is not divisible when the final stage is the essential element of the bargain.

K & G Construction Co. v. Harris (1960)

Facts: K & G Construction, a contractor, hired Harris, a subcontractor, pursuant to a contract that required Harris to perform in a "workmanlike manner." Harris breached this requirement by negligently demolishing a wall, and the company refused to pay him. K & G Construction sued for its loss after it had to pay another subcontractor an additional sum to finish the work.

Issue: Are mutual promises dependent or independent promises?

Rule: Covenants are construed as dependent or independent according to the intention of the parties and the good sense of the case. The failure of a contractor (subcontractor) to perform in a workmanlike manner may justify an owner's (contractor's) refusal to make a progress payment.

Note: The modern rule holds there is a presumption that mutual promises in a contract are dependent and are to be so regarded, whenever possible.

Hochster v. De La Tour (1853)

Facts: After De La Tour repudiated an employment contract before the contract was to commence, Hochster, the employee, brought suit for breach of contract.

Issue: May a repudiating party be sued before his performance is due under the contract?

Rule: Renunciation of a contract to do a future act may be treated as a breach of contract, and the repudiating party can be sued before his performance is due under the contract.

Phelps v. Herro (1957)

Facts: Herro contracted to transfer interests in real estate and stocks to Phelps, in exchange for $5,000 and a promissory note for the remainder to be paid in yearly installments. After Herro conveyed his interests, Phelps refused to issue the note. Herro sued for the installments though they were not yet due.

Issue: Does the doctrine of anticipatory repudiation apply to situations where the payment of money is the only obligation still due?

Rule: The doctrine of anticipatory repudiation has no application to simple unilateral contracts (or bilateral contracts that have become unilateral by full performance on one side) for the payment of money in the future, without surety or other conditions involved. Suit can only be brought at the time set for performance.

McCloskey & Co. v. Minweld Steel Co. (1955)

Facts: Minweld Steel contracted to supply and erect steel for the construction of hospitals. Due to the outbreak of the Korean War, Minweld Steel was unable to obtain the steel and asked for assistance from McCloskey & Co, the plaintiffs. Although Minweld Steel stated that they "were anxious . . . that there be no delay in the final completion of the buildings," McCloskey sued for anticipatory breach.

Issue: Does a request for help in fulfilling contractual obligations amount to an anticipatory breach absent a positive statement of unwillingness to perform?

Rule: To give rise to a renunciation amounting to a breach of contract, there must be an absolute and unequivocal refusal to perform or a distinct and positive statement of an inability to do so. The court also stated that failure to take preparatory action before the time when any performance is promised is not an anticipatory breach.

Bill's Coal Co. v. Board of Public Utilities, Etc. (1982) Note Case

Facts: The Board of Public Utilities had a contract to purchase coal from Bill's Coal. The contract provided that the Board could terminate the contract if it could find another supplier who charged at least 15% less. The contract was unclear on the method for such a price comparison, although the coal company's interpretation was ridiculous.

Issue: Is a bad faith interpretation of a contractual term a repudiation of the contract?

Rule: The bad faith urging of an interpretation of a contractual term is neither a failure to perform contract obligations (breach) nor an indication those obligations will not be performed in the future (repudiation).

Cosden Oil & Chem. Co. v. Karl O. Helm Aktiengesellschaft (1984)

Facts: Cosden Oil anticipatorily breached a contract to sell and deliver polystyrene to Helm. In assessing Helm's damages, the jury ruled that its subsequent purchases did not "cover" for the polystyrene Cosden Oil was to have supplied. Helm was entitled to the difference between market and contract prices.
Issue: If an anticipatory breach occurs, which market price is used to measure damages?
Rule: Buyer's damages after a seller's repudiation are measured at a commercially reasonable time after the buyer learns of the repudiation (UCC §§ 2-713, 2-610), but before the time for performance arrives.

United States v. Seacoast Gas Co. (1953)

Facts: Seacoast contracted with the Government to supply gas to a federal housing project. On October 7, 1947 the defendant sent a letter stating that it intended to cease performance of the contract as of November 15 of that year. The Government sought to cover, accepting a bid from Trion Company on November 10. Before the Government signed the new contract, however, Seacoast mailed a written retraction of its repudiation.
Issue: May a party retract its notice of repudiation?
Rule: A party may retract its anticipatory breach prior to a change of position by the other party. In the instant case, the Government substantially changed its position when it accepted Trion's bid on November 10; thus, Seacoast's retraction was ineffectual.

Iron Trade Prod. Co. v. Wilkoff Co. (1922)

Facts: Wilkoff Co. was to supply Iron Trade Products with rails. Since there were only a few rail suppliers, Iron Trade Products' substantial purchases from parties with whom Wilkoff had been negotiating reduced the supply and drove up the price which caused it to refuse to perform.

Issue: May a party refuse to perform if the performance of his contractual obligations has been made more difficult by the actions of the other party?
Rule: Mere difficulty of performance will not excuse a breach of contract. A seller's duty to supply goods is not excused if the buyer's additional purchases of the goods elsewhere makes them scarce and difficult to obtain.

Pittsburgh-Des Moines Steel Co. v. Brookhaven Manor Water Co. (1976)

Facts: Pittsburgh-Des Moines Steel (PDM) contracted to build a water tank for Brookhaven. Although Brookhaven was not required to pay until the work was completed, PDM requested that the money be placed in escrow or that its president would personally guarantee the payment, after it heard incorrect rumors that Brookhaven was in financial difficulties. When Brookhaven refused to do either, PDM sued for anticipatory breach.
Issue: Are rumors of financial difficulties sufficient grounds for insecurity with respect to the other party's ability to perform its obligations?
Rule: UCC § 2-609 allows a party to ask for adequate assurance of due performance and suspend its own performance until it receives such assurance only when reasonable grounds for insecurity arise with respect to the other party's performance. Here, there were no reasonable grounds for PDM to invoke this section.

Phoenix Ins. Co. v. Ross Jewelers, Inc., (1966) Note Case

Facts: Burglars cut their way into a retail store operated by Ross Jewelers and made off with $60,000 in merchandise. The insurance policy required Ross Jewelers to use a protective vault but the manager left the key in the lock. Ross Jewelers also violated a provision of the policy requiring that a detailed inventory of the store's property be kept. The insurance company wrote a letter stating that it would not pay for anything stolen from the vault but it did authorize a settlement for the remainder of the stolen goods. However, after Ross Jewelers brought suit, the insurance company disclaimed all liability relying on the inventory clause.
Issue: Can a party waive a defense to breach?

Rule: Waiver depends upon intention, the intention may be inferred from acts and conduct. The insurance company waived its defense under the inventory clause after it first denied liability on the sole grounds of the improper maintenance of the vault.

New England Structures, Inc. v. Loranger (1968)

Facts: Loranger, a general contractor, sent a telegram informing New England Structures, a subcontractor, that it was terminating the contract within five days because New England had failed to provide a sufficient amount of skilled workmen. In a suit for damages, Loranger later claimed New England had done defective work.

Issue: Where a party gives a reason for its action for breach of contract, is it estopped from asserting different grounds after litigation has begun?

Rule: A party is not estopped from asserting grounds not mentioned originally to the other party unless the other party establishes that it relied to its detriment upon the assertion. Detrimental reliance exists if the other party would have been able to cure the non-listed defects.

McKenna v. Vernon (1917) Note Case

Facts: McKenna constructed a movie theatre for Vernon. The contract called for payments to be made in installments upon the condition that an architect certify the work was being done. Vernon paid McKenna on several occasions without requiring an architect's certificate but later claimed he was not liable for the rest of the money in the absence of a certificate from the architect of final completion of the building.

Issue: If a party repeatedly disregards a provision of a contract, may it later assert that provision as a defense?

Rule: A party may not assert a provision of a contract as a defense when it has repeatedly waived the provision by its actions.

Britton v. Turner (1834)

Facts: Britton breached a 12-month employment contact without reason after completing 9 1/2 months.

Issue: Is a party who voluntarily breaches an employment contract entitled to recover anything for the labor actually performed?

Rule: Although not entitled to recover on the contract itself, a defaulting plaintiff may receive the reasonable value of his services less the damages incurred by the other party. In determining the reasonable value of services the contract price cannot be exceeded.

Kirkland v. Archbold (1953)

Facts: Kirkland defaulted after only partially completing the repairs and improvements required under a contract to work on Archbold's house.

Issue: Can a breaching party who has bestowed some benefit on the other party recover for the value of his part performance?

Rule: A defaulting contractor who has materially enriched the estate of the other contracting party may receive the reasonable value of the work done, less whatever damage the other party has suffered.

Chapter 8

IMPRACTICABILITY AND FRUSTRATION

After a valid contract has been made by the parties, unforeseen developments may make performance of the contract impossible or of no value to one of the parties. In such situations, courts may excuse nonperformance of a party's contractual duties on the grounds of impossibility, impracticability or frustration. These doctrines can be used as defenses by a party who seemingly breaches or refuses to perform.

I. IMPOSSIBILITY GENERALLY

A. Effect

Contractual duties are discharged if their performance becomes impossible.

1. Temporary impossibility does not completely discharge performance, but suspends it until the impossibility ends.

2. If performance is partially impossible, contractual duties are only discharged to the extent that the impossibility applies.

B. Allocation of Risk

If the parties have expressly allocated the risk of the occurrence of the impossibility, or surrounding circumstances or the conduct of the parties suggest that one party should bear the risk (implied allocation), then the excuse of impossibility is unavailable. In other words, if the contingency is sufficiently foreseeable, it will be included among the parties' contractual risks.

C. Timing

The impossibility must arise after the contract has been formed. Impossibility that results from circumstances existing at the time of the contract (i.e., one of the parties knows that performance of the other's duties will be impossible, but makes the contract anyhow) is treated as fraud or mistake.

D. Objective Test

Courts usually require that performance must be objectively impossible. It must be impossible for anyone to perform, not just the defendant. Exceptions:

1. Where a party cannot perform due to insolvency, it does not matter that a solvent party could have performed.

2. In contracts for personal services, the death of the party required to render the services will dissolve the contract.

E. If performance of a collateral provision is impossible, courts are less likely to excuse nonperformance than if an essential element was involved.

1. Courts require that a party must utilize an alternative mode of performance to satisfy the collateral provision.

2. UCC § 2-614 provides for use of reasonable alternative methods of delivery or payment if those provided for in the contract become impossible to perform.

II. WHEN IMPOSSIBILITY DISCHARGES PERFORMANCE

A. Traditional View

Prior to the Nineteenth century, courts did not recognize impossibility as an excuse for nonperformance. The rationale was that a contingency could always have been provided for in the contract.

B. Modern View

If subject matter essential to the performance of the contract is destroyed through no fault of the parties, the contract will be discharged.

1. Construction

If a party contracts to construct a building, he is not ordinarily excused from performance if the building is destroyed through no fault of his own. The builder is said to have assumed the risk of any construction problems.

2. Repair
   A party that contracts to repair an existing structure is discharged if the structure is destroyed. The structure to have been repaired is considered to be the "essential subject matter of the agreement," and its existence was a "basic assumption" on which the contract was made.

3. Sale of Goods Contracts (UCC)
   If the contract involves specifically identified goods that are destroyed or damaged through no fault of either party, and the buyer has not assumed the risk of such damage, the contract is discharged if the loss is total. In cases of partial damage, the buyer can choose to either void the entire contract or accept the goods with due reduction from the contract price for the damaged goods. (UCC § 2-613.)

   a. It is essential that the goods be specifically described in the contract and be unique in some way; otherwise, impossibility will not apply because substitutes are available.

   b. If an agreed source of supply is destroyed, nonperformance is excused.

   c. Goods not Identified
      If the contract requires the seller to provide goods from his inventory without specifying the goods and the goods are destroyed, the seller is excused if their existence was a basic assumption of the contract. (UCC § 2-615.)

   d. If the shipping terms are "free on board seller's plant," the risk of destruction of the goods is shifted from the seller to the buyer once the goods are placed with the carrier. If seller makes a destination contract ("free on board buyer's business"), risk is shifted only after the buyer receives the goods.

C. Supervening Illegality

A contract that was valid when entered into may be rendered illegal by a subsequent change in the law. This "supervening illegality" is frequently treated as a form of impossibility that discharges performance.

D. Defective Specifications

1. If a buyer/owner prepares defective contract specifications, the manufacturer/contractor is usually excused from performance.

2. If the manufacturer/contractor prepares defective specifications, he is not excused from performance.

E. Third Party's Failure to Perform

1. If a third party's performance or a particular source of supply is either contractually required or assumed to be part of the agreement, performance is discharged if the third party or source of supply cannot perform.

2. The nonperforming party must employ all due measures to try to assure himself that the third party or source of supply will not fail. (UCC § 2-615, Comment 4.)

3. If a third party's performance or a particular source of supply is not contractually required and not assumed to be part of the agreement, performance is not discharged.

III. IMPRACTICABILITY

Modern courts will discharge duties that are commercially impracticable to perform, even though they may be possible.

A. Test to determine impracticability

1. An extreme and unreasonable obstacle hinders performance, and

2. The obstacle was unforeseen at the time the contract was made.

B. Performance is discharged if;

1. It is rendered impracticable, without fault of one of the parties, by the occurrence of an event,

2. The nonoccurrence of the event was a "basic assumption" on which the contract was made, and

3. The party did not expressly or impliedly assume the risk of the occurrence. (Rest. 2d. § 261.)

C. Sale of Goods Context
Nondelivery or delay in delivery by a seller is not a breach if

1. Performance as agreed has been made impracticable by the occurrence of a contingency,

2. The nonoccurrence of that contingency was a basic assumption on which the contract was made, and

3. The seller did not assume a "greater obligation" (i.e., did not assume the risk of unforeseen developments).

D. Increased Costs

1. Increased costs are not usually grounds for impracticability unless the cost increase is extreme and the nonperforming party did not assume the risk of its occurrence.

2. Comment 4 to UCC § 2-615
Increased cost alone does not excuse performance unless the rise in cost is due to some unforeseen contingency which alters the essential nature of the performance.

a. Severe shortage of supplies due to war, embargo, local crop failure, or unforeseen shutdown of sources of supply usually warrants nonperformance.

b. Neither a rise nor collapse in market prices is in itself a justification.

c. Entire-enterprise Test
In determining whether the negative impact of a price increase is sufficient to render performance impracticable, some courts look to the overall profitability of the organization, including earnings from contracts with other parties.

IV. FRUSTRATION OF PURPOSE

If the essential purpose of a contract is frustrated, each party's duty of performance is discharged, even if performance is not impossible.

A. Elements (Rest. 2d. § 265)

1. A party's principal reason for making the contract is substantially frustrated by a supervening event.

2. Non-occurrence of the event was a basic assumption upon which the contract was made.

3. The party did not expressly or impliedly assume the risk of the occurrence.

B. Sale of Goods

Frustration of purpose is included under the UCC § 2-615 provisions (see commercial impracticability, above).

V. REMEDIES (Apply to all three doctrines.)

A. Restitution and reliance recovery are allowed for part performance prior to discharge of contractual duties. (Rest. 2d. § 377.) The party receives the contract rate or the reasonable value of the part performance.

B. Generally, there is no recovery for reliance that has not conferred a benefit on the other party. However, Restatement (Second) § 272(2) opposes the general rule and allows relief "as justice requires," including protection of the parties' reliance interests.

C. Reformation
Instead of dissolving a contract whose principal purpose has become frustrated, impossible, or impracticable, some courts will reform the problematic provisions and make the contract performable.

CASE CLIPS

Taylor v. Caldwell (1863)

Facts: The plaintiff contracted to rent the defendant's concert hall. The defendant was unable to convey the hall because it had burnt down through no fault of his own. The plaintiff claimed that the defendant breached the contract and brought suit to recover advertising expenses.
Issue: Are both parties excused from performance if that which was essential to their performance ceased to exist?
Rule: In contracts in which performance depends on the continued existence of a given person or thing, there is an implied condition that impossibility of performance arising from the destruction of the person or thing excuses performance.

Transatlantic Fin. Corp. v. United States (1956)

Facts: Transatlantic was forced to sail 3,000 additional miles to deliver U.S. wheat because the Suez Canal was closed due to war. After receiving only the contract price, Transatlantic sued in *quantum meruit* (ie., for what it deserved) for the extra expense.

Issue: Will added expense excuse performance of a contract under the doctrine of impossibility?
Rule: Increased cost will not render performance of a contract legally impossible. The impossibility requires that an unexpected contingency occurred, the risk of the occurrence was not allocated, either by agreement or custom, and the occurrence of the contingency rendered performance commercially impracticable, or possible only by excessive and unreasonable cost.
Note: In the instant case, the plaintiff claimed that the closure of the canal made the agreement impossible to perform, and that use of the new route required a new contract. However, the court ruled that there was no contractual requirement to use the Suez Canal.

Canadian Indus. Alcohol v. Dunbar Molasses Co. (1932) Note Case

Facts: Dunbar contracted to supply Canadian with 1,500,000 gallons of molasses. Dunbar could only deliver 344,000 gallons because the refinery both parties relied on had to cut back production. Dunbar did not have a contract with the refinery to guarantee him a minimum supply.
Issue: Is a party excused from delivering contracted for goods if its supplier reduces output to an insufficient level?
Rule: A party's nonperformance will not be excused if he impliedly bears the risk of the performance becoming difficult.

Waldinger Corp. v. CRS Group Engineers, Inc. (1985)

Facts: Ashbrook subcontracted to build sludge dewatering equipment for Waldinger, a general contractor. CRS prepared mechanical and performance specifications for the facilities and required that any equipment supplied meet both sets of specifications. Ashbrook discovered that equipment in strict compliance with the mechanical specifications would not meet performance requirements, but CRS would not waive the mechanical specifications as is often done in the industry.
Issue: Will nonperformance be excused on the grounds of commercial impracticability where a party unreasonably insists on irreconcilable requirements?
Rule: Nonperformance is excused on the grounds of commercial impracticability if a promisor insists on irreconcilable specifications.

Eastern Airlines v. Gulf Oil Corp. (1975)

Facts: Despite rising oil prices, the defendant could not raise the price of the oil it supplied the plaintiff due to federal regulations.
Issue: Will cost increases excuse performance?
Rule: Cost increases will excuse nonperformance due to commercial impracticability under UCC § 2-615 only if it is "positively unjust to hold the parties bound."
Note: Here, it was not unjust, because the volatility of the oil market was foreseeable and could have been provided against in the contract. Furthermore, Gulf failed to prove any hardship was endured.

Mineral Park Land Co. v. Howard (1916) Note Case

Facts: The defendant contracted to obtain its gravel and sand needs from the plaintiff's land, but stopped performing when it reached sand and gravel below water level, which made removing operations much more costly.
Issue: May nonperformance be excused if the cost of performance becomes extremely high?
Rule: Performance of a contract premised on the assumption that goods are available can be excused for impracticability if excessive cost has the practical result of making the goods unavailable.

Eastern Airlines, Inc. v. McDonnell Douglas Corp. (1976) Note Case

Facts: McDonnell Douglas breached a series of contracts to build planes for Eastern by delivering late. It blamed these delays on informal government requests to give priority to military orders needed for Vietnam but was not allowed to introduce evidence that these requests were the cause of the delay. The informal requests contained an implied threat of formal sanctions to compel placing priority on military orders. The contract contained an excusable delay clause which included, but was not limited to, delay due to government priorities.
Issue 1: Does UCC § 2-615 prohibit parties from contracting to expand or limit the excuses available to a promisor for nonperformance?
Rule 1: Parties may contract to narrow or broaden excuses available to a promisor.

Issue 2: Does UCC § 2-615, which excuses delay when agreed upon performances have been rendered commercially "impracticable," require that an event be unforeseeable at the time the agreement was executed?
Rule 2: Section 2-615 may apply even when the superseding event is foreseeable if the circumstances causing the breach have made performance so different from what was anticipated that the contract cannot reasonably govern.

Krell v. Henry (1903)

Facts: Henry placed a deposit on a room to be rented to watch the king's coronation. When the coronation was canceled, he refused to pay the balance owed for the rental of the room.
Issue: Are duties under a contract discharged if the essential purpose of the contract is frustrated?
Rule: If the essential purpose for contracting is frustrated, each party's duty of performance is discharged, even if performance is not impossible (i.e., the defendant can still rent the room).

Swift Canadian Co. v. Banet (1955)

Facts: Banet contracted to buy lamb pelts from Swift, but later notified Swift that he would not accept any additional shipments because new federal regulations prevented the importation of pelts into the United States. The contract provided that neither party was liable for acts of the government and that the goods were sold "F.O.B. seller's plant."
Issue: Can a party recover for breach of contract if the other party refuses to perform due to frustration of profitability?
Rule: A party ready to perform its part of a bargain is entitled to the value of the contract if the other party, which refuses to perform because profitability has been frustrated, bears the risk of loss.
Note: Here, the court found that the risk of loss shifted to the buyer when the seller became ready to perform.

Northern Indiana Pub. Serv. Co. v. Carbon County Coal Co. (1986)

Facts: NIPSCO, a public utility, entered into a long-term fixed-price contract to buy coal from Carbon County. New government regulations required that if NIPSCO could acquire electric power from other

suppliers at lower costs, it must charge its customers accordingly, even if it paid higher prices for Carbon County coal. The contract contained a clause that provided that NIPSCO could stop taking delivery of coal for any cause beyond its control, including acts of civil authority, which wholly or partly prevent utilizing the coal. The plaintiff tried to escape the contract on grounds that it was commercially impracticable to perform.
Issue: Is a buyer relieved from performance on the grounds of impracticability if the risk has been allocated to it through a fixed-price contract term?
Rule: A party is not excused from performance on the grounds of impracticability if it accepted the risk of a fixed-price term.

Young v. City of Chicopee (1904)

Facts: Young was hired to repair a bridge which was subsequently destroyed by fire without fault of either party. Young sued to recover for work completed and unused materials destroyed in the fire.
Issue: Is an owner liable for work completed and materials bought in preparation for future work if the object of the contract is destroyed without fault of either party?
Rule: If a structure upon which work is to be done is destroyed absent either party's fault, the owner is liable for work that has been completed but not for unused materials.

J.J. Brooksbank Co., Inc. v. Budget Rent-a-Car Corp. (1983)

Facts: For nearly ten years, Budget provided Brooksbank, pursuant to their franchise agreement, with one-third of its reservations for cars free of charge. Technological advancements allowed Budget to centralize the system. Following these advances, Budget attempted to charge Brooksbank for all reservations.
Issue: May a party be excused from performance on the basis of impracticability due to technological change if such was not expressly accounted for in the contract?
Rule: If a substantial change occurs in a relationship, the agreement may be adapted to the new realities of their arrangement consistent with the original contract, but a party will not be excused from its obligations as a result of technological change.
Note: The court ruled that Budget is obligated to continue to provide Brooksbank with a discount of one-third off reservation costs.

Chapter 9

THIRD PARTY BENEFICIARIES

Generally, contracts between two parties only confer benefits on the parties. Sometimes, two parties may make a contract for the benefit of a third party. The overriding issue in these cases is who is entitled to sue in case of breach. Example: A pays C to sing for B. If C does not sing, can B, the third party beneficiary, sue C? Can A sue C?

I. INTENDED V. INCIDENTAL BENEFICIARIES

Only an intended third party beneficiary is entitled to sue if the contract made for his benefit is breached.

A. Intended Beneficiary

To conclude that a third party was intended to be a beneficiary, courts must determine that this would effectuate the intentions of the parties, and either

1. The obligee was to pay money to the beneficiary, or

2. Circumstances indicate that the promisee intended to give the beneficiary the benefit of the promised performance, as indicated by the following factors:

   a. Whether the beneficiary is named in the contract

   b. Whether performance was to be made directly to the beneficiary

   c. Whether the beneficiary can change the terms of the performance

   d. Whether the beneficiary could have reasonably relied on the contract

B. Incidental Beneficiary

Although an incidental beneficiary receives the benefits of a contract made between other parties, he is not entitled to sue if that contract is breached because it was not intended that he receive any benefits. A party is an incidental beneficiary if he does not satisfy the standards of an intended beneficiary. Example: A contracts with State to build a new exit for the highway. B owns a gas station near the site of the new exit. The new exit will be beneficial to B's business, but he is only an incidental beneficiary of the contract.

II. TYPES OF BENEFICIARIES

Traditionally, there were two types of beneficiaries.

A. Creditor Beneficiary

If a party contracts with a second party to repay the first party's debt to a third party, the third party is called a creditor beneficiary. Example: A owes B $100. C owes A $100. To satisfy his debt with A, C promises A that he will pay B (the creditor beneficiary) $100. Note: The creditor (B) always retains the right to sue the original debtor (A).

B. Donee Beneficiary

If a party contracts with a second party to confer a benefit on a third party, the third party is called a donee beneficiary. Example: B promises A to give C $1,000 from A's estate at A's death. Note: The donee beneficiary (C) does not have a right to sue the promisee (A), but may sue the promisor in case of breach.

C. Restatement (Second) § 302

The traditional "creditor" and "donee" categories have been eliminated. All beneficiaries are classified as intended or incidental.

III. LAWSUITS IN BENEFICIARY CUSTOMS

Lawsuits arise when the promisor fails to confer the agreed upon benefit to the intended beneficiary.

A. Intended Beneficiary v. Promisor

1. The promisor's defenses include any defenses which could have been raised if the promisor were sued by the promisee (no mutual assent, failure of consideration, etc.).

2. The promisor cannot raise any claims that the beneficiary and the promisee may have against each other because the promisor's rights and obligations stem only from the contract with the promisee.

3. Exception: If the promise was qualified, such that the promisor agreed to make payment "only if the promisee was indebted to the beneficiary," then the promisor may prove that there was no debt.

B. Intended Beneficiary v. Promisee

1. If the benefit is not conferred onto the beneficiary, that party cannot bring suit against the promisee because they are not involved in a contractual relationship.

2. Exception: A creditor beneficiary may sue the promisee directly on the original contract lending to the promisee.

C. Promisee v. Promisor

A promisee may bring suit against a promisor to enforce a promise that would benefit a third-party beneficiary.

IV. MODIFICATION OF A BENEFICIARY'S RIGHTS

A. After a contract has been made for the benefit of a third party, the contracting parties may usually modify or rescind the contract, denying the benefit to the intended third party, unless:

1. The contract expressly states that it cannot be modified, or

2. The contract is silent on the issue of modification and the third party has materially relied on it, brought suit to enforce it, or manifested assent to it.

B. The beneficiary is entitled to any consideration the promisee gets from the promisor for an ineffective attempt to modify the contract.

CASE CLIPS

Lawrence v. Fox (1859)

Facts: Mr. Holly owed Lawrence $300. Holly loaned Fox $300 on condition that he repay the $300 to Lawrence, in satisfaction of Holly's debt. Fox did not pay.
Issue: Can a third party creditor-beneficiary sue to enforce a contract between two other parties that was made for the benefit of the third party?
Rule: A third party can sue to enforce an agreement between two other parties which was made for the benefit of the third party even though there is no privity with the third party.

Seaver v. Ransom (1918)

Facts: Mrs. Beman was about to die and wanted to change her will to provide for her niece, Seaver. Because Mrs. Beman was afraid she would die before a new will could be written, her husband promised that he would provide for the niece at his death if the will was left unchanged. At his death Mr. Beman left nothing for Seaver, who sued his administrator.
Issue: May third party donee-beneficiary enforce a promise made between two others for its benefit?
Rule: A party may enforce a contract made for its benefit by two other parties. Third-party beneficiaries are an exception to the requirement of privity between contracting parties.

Lucas v. Hamm (1961)

Facts: Hamm, an attorney, prepared a will for his client. After the will was probated, a provision was declared invalid because of an error made by Hamm. The plaintiffs sued Hamm because they received $75,000 less than they would have received had the provision been valid.

Issue: May an intended beneficiary of a will sue an attorney for improperly drawing the will?

Rule: When the main purpose and intent of a testator in making his agreement with an attorney is to benefit a third party named in the will, as a matter of policy the intended beneficiaries may recover as third party beneficiaries in the event of the attorney's breach.

Lonsdale v. Chesterfield (1983)

Facts: Chesterfield subdivided and sold parcels of land. Each sales contract contained a clause stating that Chesterfield would install a water system, which was to be paid for by the owners of the parcel. Chesterfield sold its interest to Sansaria. A clause in their contract provided that Sansaria would install the water system, but it did not. Purchasers of the subdivisions sued to enforce the agreement between Sansaria and Chesterfield.

Issue: May a party enforce a contract between two other parties if it is to benefit from the contract.

Rule: Third parties who benefit from a contract between two others may enforce the contract, provided the parties to the contract intended that one party assume a direct obligation to the third party.

Cretex Companies, Inc. v. Construction Leaders, Inc. (1984)

Facts: Construction Leaders, a general contractor, was issued a performance bond by Travelers Indemnity for two construction projects. Cretex, a supplier of materials, was not paid when the general contractor defaulted. Cretex sued both Construction Leaders and Travelers Indemnity for damages.

Issue: When is a third party an "intended beneficiary?"

Rule: Under the Restatement (Second) § 302, if recognition of third party beneficiary rights is "appropriate" and either the duty owed or the intent to benefit test is met, the third party can recover as an "intended beneficiary." Subcontractors do not meet this standard when attempting to recover from a surety on a defaulting general contractor's performance bond.

Davis v. United Air Lines (1983)

Facts: Davis, an epileptic, sued his employer, United Air Lines, for wrongful dismissal from his job. An applicable federal statute required all parties contracting with the United States to take affirmative action to employ qualified handicapped individuals but the statute did not provide for a private right of action.

Issue: When the parties to a contract manifest an intent to benefit a third party, may that party still be denied a remedy if it is inappropriate?

Rule: Under the Restatement (Second) § 302, a third party beneficiary cannot enforce a contract between two others unless allowing such enforcement is "appropriate to effectuate the intention of the parties." The parties to this contract did not intend for third parties to bring such an action.

Rouse v. United States (1954)

Facts: Winston signed a promissory note for construction of a heating system in her house. The United States eventually took assignment of the note. Rouse bought Winston's house agreeing to assume Winston's debt, but failed to make payments. The United States sued to enforce the contract, claiming it was a third-party beneficiary. Rouse defended that Winston fraudulently misrepresented the condition of the heating plant and that it had not been properly installed and, thus, the United States did not deserve to be paid.

Issue: What defenses can be raised against a third-party beneficiary?

Rule: A party which promises to make a payment to another party's creditor can assert any defense against the creditor that it could have asserted had it been sued by the promisee. If a promisor's agreement is to be interpreted as a promise to discharge whatever liability the promisee is under, the promisor is allowed to show that the promisee was not actually liable (because of improper performance by the third party). However, when the promise was to pay a certain amount of money to the promisee's creditor, it is immaterial to challenge whether the promisee is actually indebted.

Detroit Bank & Trust Co. v. Chicago Flame Hardening Co., Inc. (1982)

Facts: Three partners made a contract to provide a cash stipend to their spouses in case of their death. The agreement was later rescinded, but one of the spouses challenged the rescission after her husband died.

Issue: May a contract be modified or rescinded to the detriment of a third-party beneficiary?

Rule: A contract may be modified or rescinded to the detriment of a third party beneficiary at any time before the contract is accepted, adopted or acted upon by the third party beneficiary.

Karo v. San Diego Symphony Orchestra Ass'n (1985)

Facts: The collective bargaining agreement between the symphony and its union provided that vacant chairs in the orchestra be filled through "blind" auditions. The two parties modified the agreement and Karo, a musician, sued when a chair was filled without an audition.

Issue: When may the parties modify a contract to the detriment of a third party beneficiary?

Rule: The power to modify terminates when the third party beneficiary materially changes position in justifiable reliance on the promise before receiving notification of the modification.

Chapter 10

ASSIGNMENT AND DELEGATION

Assignment and delegation involve the transfer of contractual rights or duties to a third party. The issues that usually arise involve questions of which rights/duties are transferable, what are the consequences of such transfers for the original parties, and what is the extent of the third party's obligations.

I. DEFINITIONS

A. Assignment
A party to a contract (assignor) transfers contractual rights to a third person (assignee).

B. Delegation
A party to a contract (obligor/promisor) transfers contractual duties to a third person (delegatee).

C. Assignment and Delegation v. Third-Party Beneficiary v. Novation

1. Assignment and delegation occur after a contract is executed. There is no requirement that both parties agree to it.

2. Third-party beneficiaries are created at the time the contract is made.

3. Novations occur when both parties agree that a third party substitute for one party.

II. ASSIGNMENT

A. An assignment is a present transfer of contractual rights. A promise to transfer contractual rights at a future date is not an assignment. UCC Article 9 covers many assignments.

B. Rights That May Be Assigned

Generally, all contractual rights are assignable, with the following exceptions:

Mnemonic: **POP FRED**

1. **P**rohibited by law
2. **OP**tion to enter a bilateral contract that is accompanied by an impermissible delegation of duties
3. **F**uture rights
4. **R**isks to obligor are substantially altered
5. **E**xpress agreement prohibiting assignment
6. **D**uty of obligor would be altered

1. **P**rohibited by Law

   A right cannot be assigned if a statute or public policy prohibits the assignment of that type of right. The most common examples are rights to future alimony payments, torts claims that are assigned to lawyers, and rights to wages.

2. **Op**tions

   a. Unilateral options may be assigned. Example: Joe tells Moe, "If you give me $250,000 within 30 days, I will sell you my house." Moe can assign the option to Bo.

   b. Options for bilateral contracts can only be assigned if unaccompanied by an impermissible delegation. Example: Joe tells Moe, "I will give you 30 days to promise me that you will buy my house for $250,000 and also play tuba at my wedding as part of the deal." Moe can assign his right (option) to Bo, but Bo's acceptance is only valid if Moe, not Bo, plays the tuba (a duty) at Joe's wedding. Note: See "Delegation" for more on impermissible delegations.

3. **F**uture Rights

   Rights that are expected to arise in the future are not assignable. An attempt to make a present assignment of future rights has the effect of a promise to assign the rights when they do arise. If the assignment is based on an existing contract, however, it is enforceable. Example: B, a buyer, assigns the rights to future deliveries he will receive from S, a seller, under their present contract. The assignment would be shaky if B promises to assign future deliveries from a contract he hopes/expects to make with S in a few months.

4. Risk to Obligor Substantially Altered
   Assignment is not permitted if the obligor's risk will be materially changed as a result. Risks do not have to be increased, just altered. Example: S sells a plane to B and attempts to assign the insurance policy on it. The assignment is ineffective because the policy is based on the age, experience, etc., of the pilot which varies from person to person.

5. Express Contractual Clause not to Assign
   A general clause prohibiting assignment will not usually invalidate an assignment of rights under the contract. Although the assignment is effective, the assignor is held to have breached the contract. The Rest. 2d. § 322 and UCC § 2-210 provide that an express contractual clause prohibiting assignment is valid, but that subsequent assignments are breaches of the contract. The Restatement provides the following exceptions (rights assignable regardless of contrary clauses):

   a. The right to sue for breach of contract by the other party.

   b. The right to return performance where the assignor has fully performed his obligations.

   c. An anti-assignment clause is waivable by the party for whose benefit it was made.

   d. An agreement not to "assign the contract" is construed to bar delegation of duties only, not assignment of rights. However, language that clearly bars assignment will be upheld as barring assignment of rights also. (see *Allhusen v. Caristo Construction Corp.*) Note: Under UCC Article 9, which covers commercial financing, any anti-assignment term in a contract that comes within the scope of Article 9 is ineffective.

6. Duty of Obligor Altered
   Assignments that materially change an obligor's duties are prohibited.

   a. Personal Service Contracts
      Employers cannot assign rights to receive services if the services are unique or based on a special relationship.

   b. Output Contracts
      At common law, such contracts were not assignable. The UCC allows assignment of output contracts if the output of the assignee will not be unreasonably disproportionate to the assignor's expected production under the original contract.

III. REQUIREMENTS OF AN EFFECTIVE ASSIGNMENT

A. Present transfer

B. Adequate description of the right to be assigned

C. Does not have to be in writing, except for the following:

   1. Interest in land

   2. Sale of goods over $500

   3. Chose in action worth more than $5,000

   4. Security interests under UCC Article 9

   5. Wage assignments

D. Consideration is not required. However, a gratuitous assignment is revocable.

1. Automatic revocation occurs upon

   a. Death of assignor.

   b. Bankruptcy of assignor.

   c. Subsequent reassignment of the right by assignor to another person.

   d. Notice is given by assignor to assignee that the assignment has been revoked.

2. Gratuitous assignments can be made irrevocable by

   a. Delivery to the assignor of a document symbolizing the right that was assigned (stock certificate, bankbook, insurance policy, etc.).

   b. A writing, made by the assignor, providing that the assignment will not be revoked.

   c. Detrimental reliance by the assignee on the assignment.

   d. Obligor rendering the assigned performance.

   e. Giving consideration for the assignment.

IV. RIGHTS OF THE PARTIES AFTER AN ASSIGNMENT

A. Privity of contract is established between the obligor and assignee and erased between obligor and assignor.

B. Rights of the Assignee
The assignee "steps into the shoes" of the assignor and thus can directly enforce the contract.

C. Rights of the Obligor
The obligor may assert any defense against the assignee that would have been available to assert against the assignor. For example, if the assignor did not give consideration or misrepresented a material fact, this defense can be raised against the assignee's right.

D. Rights of Assignee against Assignor
If the assignee is unable to recover from the obligor, that party may try to recover from the assignor.

1. Gratuitous Assignment
   Assignee will not recover unless detrimental reliance is shown.

2. Assignment for Value
   An assignment that is given for consideration contains the following implied warranties:

   a. Assignor will not impair enforcement of the right.

   b. The right assigned is valid and all encumbrances have been disclosed.

   c. Any documents that evidence the transferred right are valid.

   d. The assignor does not warrant the credit-worthiness of the obligor unless the assignor expressly agrees to guarantee it.

E. Rights of Sub-assignees
If an assignee assigns the right to yet another party, all of the implied warranties of the original assignor are not automatically transferred unless the original assignor makes an express agreement. However, the sub-assignee is responsible for the transferred duties.

V. MODIFICATION OF THE CONTRACT BY THE OBLIGOR AND ASSIGNOR

An obligor and assignor may attempt to modify their agreement in a way that will affect the assignee's rights. The effect of such modification depends on the extent of the obligor's awareness of the assignee:

A. Modification Before Obligor Receives Notice of the Assignment

The obligor and assignor can modify in good faith. (Rest. 2d § 318.)

B. Modification After Obligor Receives Notice of the Assignment

The assignor and obligor can only make a "good faith" modification if the assignor has not fully performed all duties under the contract.

VI. DELEGATION OF DUTIES

Delegation involves the transfer of contractual duties. Unlike an assignor, a delegator remains liable under the contract should the delegatee improperly perform his duties.

A. Nondelegable Types of Duties

1. Contracts involving performance requiring special skills. A contract is delegable, despite a personal preference of the obligee that the original obligor perform, if the services do not require a special skill.

2. "Special trust" relationships (e.g., doctor-patient).

3. Contract provision expressly prohibits delegation.

B. Rights and Duties After Delegation

1. Obligee must accept services that were lawfully delegated.

2. The delegator remains liable for performance after delegation unless the obligee specifically consented to the delegation, thus forming a novation.

3. The Delegatee

    a. Delegation
    Delegatee may perform the duties at his option.

    b. Assumption
    Delegatee must perform because he agreed to do so in exchange for consideration. The obligor becomes a third-party beneficiary to delegatee's agreement to perform.

    c. Novation
    Under a novation, all parties must agree to the new arrangement. Delegation and assumption do not have to be approved by the obligee to be valid.

CASE CLIPS

The British Waggon Co. and the Parkgate Waggon Co. v. Lea & Co. (1880)

Facts: Parkgate Waggon leased some wagons to the defendant. It was also obligated to repair and maintain the wagons. After Parkgate delegated its duties to British, the defendant refused to pay, claiming that the delegation was invalid.
Issue: Are contractual duties that are not personal delegable?
Rule: Contractual duties are delegable, absent a clause prohibiting such delegation, if the delegator was not selected with reference to his individual skill, competency, or other personal qualifications.

Lonsdale v. Chesterfield (1983)

Facts: Chesterfield subdivided and sold parcels of land. Each sales contract contained a clause stating that Chesterfield would install a water system, which was to be paid for by the owners of the parcel. Chesterfield sold his interest to Sansaria. A clause in their contract provided that Sansaria would install the water system, but he did not. The purchasers of the subdivisions sued to enforce the agreement between Sansaria and Chesterfield.

Issue: Is an assignor of the benefits of a contract released from obligations under the contract?

Rule: A party that assigns a contract passes on the benefits, not the obligations flowing from a contract; the assignor remains responsible for the fulfillment of its duties.

Carstedt v. Grindeland (1987)

Facts: Grindeland acquired the assets, trademarks, premises and staff from his father's printing business to open his own. Eight years earlier his father had obtained the exclusive right to manufacture and sell a Carstedt machine in exchange for the payment of royalties. Grindeland refused to pay royalties under his father's agreement.

Issue: Under what circumstances will a business be held liable for the debts and obligations of the business from which its assets and other elements are transferred?

Rule: A transferee business will not be held liable for the transferor business's debts and obligations unless it is designated a "continuation" of the transferor business; the designation is limited to business "reorganizations" under federal bankruptcy law or statute.

Crane Ice Cream Co. v. Terminal Freezing & Heating Co. (1925)

Facts: Frederick, an ice cream manufacturer, had a requirements contract for ice with Terminal. Terminal renewed the contract because he was satisfied with Frederick's adherence to the contract terms, which included exclusivity, financial responsibility, commercial responsibility and good faith efforts to maintain a sufficient volume of purchases. Terminal refused to honor Frederick's assignment of the contract to Crane.

Issue: Is an assignment invalid if the contract was induced by personal factors?

Rule: A contract may not be assigned if part of its inducement was based on personal factors. Parties have the right to the benefit they contemplated from the character, credit, and substance of the other party to the contract.

Note: The court was motivated largely by the fact that because this was a requirements contract, Terminal was in a vulnerable position.

Chemical Bank v. Rinden Professional Ass'n (1985)

Facts: Intertel Co. leased an office phone system to Rinden, which agreed to make monthly payments. Intertel assigned the payment rights to Chemical after Rinden waived all defenses to payment. Rinden stopped payment three years later when the phone system malfunctioned.

Issue: Can a buyer/obligor waive warranty rights against an assignee?

Rule: Under UCC § 9-206(1), a waiver of defenses against an assignee, which was made for value, in good faith, and without notice of a claim or defense given to the assignee at the time of waiver, is valid.

Michelin Tires (Canada) Ltd. v. First Nat. Bank of Boston (1981)

Facts: JCC Inc. contracted to build a storage facility for Michelin. JCC was to be paid periodically upon receiving certification that it had performed properly and paid all subcontractors. JCC assigned its payment rights to FNB. After several payments were made, Michelin discovered that JCC obtained its certifications by fraud and sued for the value of the payments. FNB was not aware of any fraud at the time it was assigned the rights.

Issue: Can an obligor recover payments made to an assignee because of fraud committed by an assignor but unknown to the assignee?

Rule: While UCC § 9-318 preserves defenses to an assignee's claims, it does not provide an obligor with a basis for an affirmative suit against an assignee with no knowledge of its assignor's fraud.

United California Bank v. Eastern Mountain Sports, Inc. (1982)

Facts: Snow Lion Co. assigned its accounts receivable to UCB. EMS refused to make full payment, requesting a set-off for defective goods that were sent to it by Snow Lion.

Issue: May an obligor reduce its payments to an assignee in the amount of the reduced value of the assignor's performance?

Rule: Under UCC § 9-318 if an assignor does not properly perform its obligations to an obligor, the obligor can reduce its payments to the

assignee by the damages attributable to the assignor's breach if the claims either arise from the contract (§ 9-318(1)(a)) or accrued before notice of the assignment was given (§ 9-318(1)(b)).
Note: The reduction in payments is called a set-off.

Allhusen v. Caristo Constr. Corp. (1952)

Facts: Caristo hired a subcontractor to paint for it. The subcontractor assigned its right to payment to a third party, which assigned it to Allhusen. A contract clause prohibited assignment of "monies due or to become due" without written permission from Caristo, and written permission was never obtained.
Issue: What is the legal effect of a contractual provision prohibiting assignment?
Rule: When clear language is used, parties may limit the assignment of benefits under a contract.

TABLE OF AUTHORITIES

Uniform Commercial Code

Restatement (Second) of Contracts

TABLE OF CASES

NOTES

NOTES

NOTES

NOTES

NOTES

ORDER FORM

Order today! All orders shipped within 24 hours of receipt.
Mail To:
SULZBURGER & GRAHAM PUBLISHING Ltd.
PO Box 20058
Park West Station, New York NY 10025
(800) 366-7086 (212) 769-9738 FAX orders: (212) 769-9675

Please send me **BLOND'S** ...

Product Description	Product Number	Casebook You Use	Price

Shipping & Handling $2.25

Total ________

Name ____________________
Address ____________________
City/State/Zip ____________________
Graduation ____________________
Day Phone ____________________

I Prefer:
❍ 5¼ inch diskettes
❍ 3½ inch diskettes

❍ Check or money order enclosed (payable to Sulzburger & Graham Publishing)
❍ MasterCard ❍ Visa ❍ American Express ❍ Optima ❍ DiscoverCard

Charge Card Number ____________________ **Expiration** __________ **Signature** __________

All orders are shipped UPS same or next business day. Delivery time will vary, based on distance from New York City. Washington/Boston corridor can expect delivery 2 working days after shipment. West Coast should allow 6 working days. Overnight, 2nd day and COD available at extra cost. We cannot deliver to PO Boxes.